How to Write a
Wedding Speech

How to Write a Wedding Speech

stuck for words?
hundreds of ways to say it best

from **confetti**.co.uk
don't get married without us...

First published in 2003
by Octopus Publishing Group,
2–4 Heron Quays,
London E14 4JP
www.conran-octopus.co.uk
Reprinted in 2003, 2004, 2005
Text copyright © 2003 Confetti Network
Book design and layout copyright
© 2003 Conran Octopus Limited
Illustrations copyright © Confetti Network

Publishing Director Lorraine Dickey
Senior Editor Katey Day
Assistant Editor Sybella Marlow
Creative Director Leslie Harrington
Designer Jeremy Tilston
Senior Production Controller Manjit Sihra

Thanks also to the staff at Confetti.co.uk,
brides, grooms, guests and Aunt Betti

ISBN 184091 308 8
Printed in Europe

Other books in this series include *Wedding Planner*;
Wedding Readings and Vows; *Wedding Readings*; *The Wedding Book
of Calm*; *The Best Man's Wedding*; *The Bridesmaid's Wedding*;
Your Daughter's Wedding and *Men at Weddings*

Contents

Let's be honest here: there are three things most guests remember about a wedding. What the bride wore; how long they had to wait before eating... and how good the speeches were.

If the last item on that list fills you with dread, then chances are you're lined up to speak at your own wedding, or that of a daughter, son or friend. Never fear, confetti is here to help.

This book is all about helping you make a good speech, easily. Instead of reprinting wordy, old-fashioned material irrelevant to your situation, we've gathered together a host of new, original ideas that you can pick and choose from.

Of course, you will need to add your own personal touches, anecdotes and asides. But we hope the following will give you lots of ideas. Use the Winning Lines (page 16) to help structure your speech and ensure a strong start, middle and end. Then select whatever suits your needs from the Sample Speeches (page 34 onwards). There is some space at the back of this book for you to make notes too.

Join all your chosen bits together and – hey presto – a wedding speech to remember for all the right reasons!

Note to fathers of the bride
Traditionally, you speak first and:
Thank anyone involved in planning (and paying for)
the wedding.
Speak proudly of your daughter and welcome the groom
into your family.
Thank everyone for coming.
Propose a toast to the bride and groom.

But you could also:
Make a joint speech with your wife.
Share the stage with a stepfather or godfather.
Simply thank everyone for coming and propose a toast.
Show a short film or candid camera shots of your
daughter as a child.

Note to grooms
Traditionally, you speak second and:
Thank the father of the bride for his (hopefully) kind comments!
Thank the wedding organizers/mums – often with bouquets.
Thank everyone for being there.
Compliment your new wife.
Toast the bridesmaids, often giving them a gift.

But you don't have to stick with tradition. You could:
Let the bride speak instead, or do the speech together.
Read out a poem that sums up how you feel about the day.
Simply toast those who helped with the wedding, but don't
make a speech.

Note to the best man

It's usually down to you to introduce each speaker at the wedding, unless there is a toastmaster to do it. Your speech comes last of all and traditionally, you:

Comment on how great the day has been, and thank the organizers again.

Entertain the room with stories of the groom's past and the stag do.

Read out telegrams and messages from absent friends.

Propose a toast to the bride and groom.

However, you could:

Make a joint speech with the ushers, other friends or the chief bridesmaid.

Perform a stunt (see page 21); a home video, slides or invent funny telegrams.

Other speakers

The bride and chief bridesmaid

Traditionally, neither the bride nor the chief bridesmaid
speak at a wedding, but more and more are choosing to do
so. In this case it is usual for the bride to speak just before
or after the groom, while the chief bridesmaid either follows
or precedes the best man.

A bride might like to:

Thank the guests for coming.
Thank the organizers, especially her parents.
Compliment her husband.
Propose a toast to the people who made it happen: parents,
ushers, bridesmaids.

A chief bridesmaid might like to:

Thank the bride for choosing her and for her gift
(if appropriate).
Tell a few anecdotes about the bride and/or the hen night.
Mention the hard work of the ushers and other bridesmaids.
Toast the bride and groom or those organizing the event.

Cardinal rules

Unaccustomed as you are, you're scheduled for a spot of speech-making. Stick to the cardinal rules and make your piece a sure-fire success.

Pick the right tone

Tone can be tricky. In making your speech, you have to fulfil certain obligations. You need to express thanks and convey affection. You need to be sincere. You need to entertain. What you don't need to do is come across as either dull and pompous – or as a failed stand-up comedian.

A speech without humour is a boring thing indeed, but a speech that sounds like Bernard Manning on an off-night can be impersonal and lacking in warmth. Be funny, but never risk giving offence.

The ideal tone to aim for is one of gentle humour and warmth, intimacy and affection. Aim for something that makes everyone feel included.

Keep it short

However fabulous your speech, the golden rule is always to leave your audience wanting more. Your performance should, as Oscar Wilde once said, 'be exquisite, and leave one unsatisfied.'

Wedding guests enjoy speeches, but don't overestimate their boredom threshold. However funny you are, if you go on too long, noisy coughing fits are sure to set in.

With speeches, less is always more and brevity really is the soul of wit. Stick to quick-fire quips rather than shaggy-dog stories; anecdotes rather than twenty-part sagas; pithy comments rather than rambling digressions. To help you get it right, time yourself when you practise.

Include everyone

Wedding speech-makers have it tough. Who else has to gain and keep the attention of an audience aged between two months and 92 years, not to mention making them laugh without offending a soul?

To make sure no one feels left out, imagine all the different types of people who might be listening to your speech and try to include something for everyone. Avoid in-jokes and make sure you explain references to people and places some listeners may not be familiar with. Be sensitive about the sensibilities of all the guests: that stag-night 'moonie' may not amuse everyone!

Don't wing it

Take time to prepare and write your speech. You don't have to scribble everything down at once – keep it on the back burner of your brain for a few weeks before the wedding and jot down ideas as they occur to you.

Ask others for anecdotes and use books and quotations, as well as your imagination, to help you create your masterpiece. Hone your performance by rehearsing, preferably with people you can rely on for honest, constructive feedback.

Pre-speech checklist

This book contains primarily wedding speech material. If you need more general advice on making a speech, try the first confetti book of speeches, available to order online at www.confetti.co.uk

Meanwhile, here's a quick checklist to run through a few days before the wedding...

• Does your speech fit the occasion? Is it light-hearted and positive?

• Have you tested it on others and asked for honest feedback?

• Have you timed it to ensure it's not too long?

• Have you been careful not to offend anyone? Or leave anyone out?

• Do you know in what order the speeches will be made and at what time?

• If there is a microphone, do you know how to use it?

• Have you written notes, in case you dry up?

• Have you checked names and how to pronounce them?

• Have you made a note of whom you need to thank, or any messages to be read out?

Cardinal sins

Wedding speeches should be memorable. But make sure guests remember your speech for the right reasons – not the fact that you mentioned the bride's three previous husbands. Here's what NOT to do...

Don't mention the war...

Certain subjects are best avoided: race and religious issues, ex-partners, relatives who refused to attend, the last-minute threat to call off the wedding.

Keep in mind that you have a mixed audience. Not everyone will know that Mr Trimble was your woodwork teacher. If an anecdote can't easily be explained, leave it out.

Swear words are a definite no-go area. The last thing you need is granny fainting at a four-letter word.

Bear in mind that causing offence in your wedding speech could be preserved for ever on video, as well as in the minds of the guests and the memories of the couple!

Finally, whatever your feelings about the couple's suitability, this is not the time to let hostility show. If you can't make a positive speech, delegate to someone who can.

Don't ramble

Being asked to speak is a compliment, so plan properly.
You need to know where you are going with your speech.
You need a definite structure: a beginning, middle and end.

Long, rambling speeches are likely to send the older guests
off to the land of nod, so keep it short. Likewise, long, drawn-
out jokes may fall flat if they take too long to tell – spare a
thought for guests' memory lapses.

Don't mumble

The cardinal sins here are swallowing your words, speaking
too fast and losing your place (in which case you may as well
admit it and get a laugh).

This is one of the few times in life when you can be
guaranteed a captive and sympathetic audience. They want
to make life easy for you, so help them. Check early on that
everyone can hear you. Speak slowly and clearly. Signal jokes
by pausing to allow everyone to laugh!

Don't get wasted

Tempting as it is to drink heavily to steady your nerves
before your speech, don't!

Adrenaline can increase the effect of alcohol, and any
evidence on videos and photos will haunt you forever.
Chances are you'll also slur your words, overstep the mark
and include all those lewd jokes you so carefully removed
on your 15th re-write.

It's their day

Bear in mind that this is the bride and groom's day, not yours. So spare a thought for the couple's blushes — don't mention anything you wouldn't want said about you. Some gentle ribbing about the groom's lack of footballing prowess might be funny. Anecdotes about his lecherous, two-timing ex-girlfriend are almost certainly going too far. If in doubt, leave it out.

Here's a quick recap of those wedding speech no-nos:

NO gags about race, religion or the groom's ex-wife.

NO swearing.

NO private jokes only a few guests will get.

NO ad-libbed off-the-cuff speeches, unless you are very, very good at it!

NO mumbling.

NO gabbling.

NO forgetting the list of people you had to thank or the telegrams you were supposed to read.

NO drinking to excess before you speak.

NO upsetting the bride and groom.

Winning lines

So you're ready to start scribbling your speech.

But that's exactly the problem: where do you start?

A good speech has a strong beginning, a meaty middle and ends on a high. That's why we've started this book with big sections on beginnings, middles and endings. Simply read through, select the sections that appeal and copy them in order. That way you've got a basic structure to work with.

Next, turn to the sample speeches. Here you'll find pages and pages of original material that you can use to fill out your own speech. Simply tailor it to suit your own occasion – and you're raring to go.

Break a leg!

Strong starts

Introduction

If you don't start strongly, guests will glaze over until the champagne toast. Try these to get you going...

Opening gambits

'I'm here to sing Paul's/Louise's praises. You'll be glad to hear, though, that I can't sing and there isn't much to praise, so fortunately this speech should be short and sweet.'

'Never before have I stood before such an impressive audience... unless you count my time in the dock/as chaplain at Wormwood Scrubs/as a steward at Millwall FC/on stage at Glastonbury...'

'Excuse me, but I'm a little nervous. Now I know what a Rowntree's jelly feels like.'

'Did anyone see that polar bear walk by just now? No? Shame, because they're such terrific ice-breakers.'

'They say good speeches are meant to be pithy, although what cranges have got to do with it, I don't know.'

'They say good speeches are meant to be short and sweet... So thanks very much for your time.'

'Ladies and gentlemen, thank you for your kind applause. Not for the first time today do I rise from a warm seat with a piece of paper in my hand...'

One-liners

'The groom was not always as handsome as this. When he was born the midwife took one look and slapped his father. He had the only pram in Bristol with shutters. In fact, he was so ugly his mum used to feed him with a catapult.'

'Jon has a face that launched a thousand ships. And a figure that ate a thousand chips.'

'Greg was always considered a handsome chap at college. He was fastidious about getting his beauty sleep – about 20 hours a day, usually.'

'Tony always used to take Janine out to dine in a secluded corner, lit only by candles. Partly because he's a romantic, but partly because he didn't want to scare her off!'

'Now he's married, Dom can really let himself go... oh, you already have!'

Anecdotes

'The first time Bill and Emily went away together, Emily wanted Bill to act as if they were married, to avoid any disapproving looks. So Bill let her carry the suitcases.'

'Was it love at first sight the night Ian and Sue met? There are several theories about this. Sue contends that it was love at first sight, but then she found out he already had a boyfriend, so she went home with Ian instead…'

'These two eventually found each other after years of trying. And, as practice makes perfect, they really must be the perfect couple.'

'Rob and I have been great mates for a long time now, and inevitably we've shared many things over the years: our AA counsellor; our probation officer; our therapist; our mums' recipes for bread sauce – and now, a top table. Who'd have thought it?'

Stunts

Prepare a slide show of photographs from the bride/groom's past. Drop your cards as the slide show starts and apologize, saying that they may be in the wrong order. Without looking at the pictures, give a running commentary. For example, accompany a photo of the groom in his primary school uniform with the comment: 'Rob's first day in his new job was a proud moment for the family…'

Write a mock school report for the groom/bride, referring to their character/behaviour at school, and relate this to today. For example, 'It says here that Louise "has a short attention span, responds poorly to authority, and doesn't suffer fools gladly". Which could be a problem, being married to Damian…'

Pretend to have a copy of the bride or groom's CV and pick out examples of their 'achievements'.

The best man can hold up a box marked Honeymoon Survival Kit, and pull out some props: a tube of Deep Heat; bandages; Spiderman mask; Chelsea shirt; Viagra…

Put together a spoof video documentary, in which you invite friends and family to share their thoughts and memories about the happy couple. For extra fun, film a couple of friends dressed up as the newly-weds, re-enacting the moment they first met.

Set pieces

The best man invites anyone in the audience who used to go out with the bride to return the keys to her flat. A string of friends in the know from the audience loudly troop up to the top table...

The best man gives a huge parcel to the bride. As she unwraps it, it becomes smaller and smaller. The parcel, in fact, contains nothing but a note saying, 'Thanks for padding my speech out for me, I've got nothing at all to say...'

Organize a sweepstake on the length of your speech. Keep asking the timekeeper how long you've taken and then – at apparently the most important part of the speech – abruptly sit down and announce that you've won.

The best man, or father of the bride, introduces a song, poem or tribute to the bride or groom from a football team or drama group or club of which they are a member.

Meaty middles

Aim to add between three and six 'fillings' to your speech sandwich. Such as…

Aaaah…

Something sentimental, without being too gushy, can be a nice touch…

'To have joy one must share it. Happiness was born a twin.' (Lord Byron)

'Absence diminishes little passions and increases great ones, just as the wind blows out a candle and fans a fire.' (La Rochefoucauld)

'Do not be afraid to love these days. Take them gently and with a consideration for eternity, but take them as your own. Have patience with your dreams and the expectations that you have, but do not defer all hope to the future for there are only so many tomorrows.' (Brian Baron)

'Keep your minds set on the future, your memories planted in the past, and always your hearts where they are right at this moment.' (Anon)

'Hold on to yesterday, but not too tightly; let loose just enough to reach tomorrow.' (Anon)

Religious references

'Thankfully our hosts, unlike those at the wedding feast at Canae, haven't insisted on saving the best wine till last! Though looking at one or two of you here today, I'm not sure you'd notice...'

'In the words of Saint Paul: "Forgive each other as soon as a quarrel begins." Which is God's way of saying never to go to sleep on an argument...'

'As the Bible says: "Who so findeth a wife, findeth a good thing." Now when I look at Jane, I can't help thinking, what a complete understatement!'

'When God created man and woman in his own image, we're told he blessed them and said: "Be fruitful and increase..." Now whatever did He mean by that?'

'Saint Paul advises us that "a husband must love his wife *as he loves himself*". Now if Jerry can pull THAT off, then Penny'll be a really lucky gal...'

Jokes

'Sam and Sally are like very different wines: Sam gets better with age, whereas Sally just gets drunk.'

'Bob used to do 40 push-ups every morning to make sure he could keep up with Kirsty. Now he needs 40 winks…'

'Paula is busy making their new home comfortable, although Mark told me he's quite happy with his chair in the King's Head.'

'There are three kinds of wedding ring: the engagement ring, the wedding ring and the suffer-ring!'

'How many bridesmaids does it take to change a light bulb? Five. One to yank it out of the socket and chuck it, and four to squabble over who's going to catch it.'

Observations

'Some say that star-sign compatibility is the secret of a happy marriage. But I don't really believe in all that stuff – which is unusual for a Scorpio…'

'Some (single) people think that marriage will limit them or hold them back. But look at James and Katie today, and you see two people whose lives have expanded and flourished in every way since they got together…'

'My gran, who's been married 50 years, says the secret of a successful marriage is give and take. I said: "You mean 50:50"? She said: "NO! You've both got to give 110 per cent"!'

Quips

'Confucius, I believe, said something very significant about the meaning of marriage. But it was in Chinese, so I'm afraid I didn't understand it.'

"Thanks for giving me away Dad" Sally said to me this morning. "Think nothing of it", I replied. "I've been trying to do it for years"!'

'Given that Jemima and I have been living together for eight years, I thought that for once we deserved to walk up an aisle that's not located in Sainsbury's.'

Asides

These are useful little remarks to allow you to comment on something topical or specific to the big day.

'Before I continue, has anyone ever been to a wedding this posh before? Even the cockroaches have got place names...'

'Today was already shaping up to be a wonderful occasion – but look outside and you'll agree that, with gorgeous sunshine in mid-November, we've been truly blessed.'

[Note handed to speaker by usher]
'And before we go any further, some important news just in: Rochdale 4, Hartlepool 2.'

'By the way, please don't worry if you hear any unusual noises during the speeches – it's only Jim's wallet groaning in agony...'

'I must say I'm surprised by today's downpour. Sarah's parents have been such terrific wedding organizers, I assumed they'd be able to control the weather too!'

On this occasion...

'It's amazing, really, that Rob ever got as far as the wedding reception. He's a terrible driver and he's never got change for the bus.'

'This occasion is rather like a football game: two raucous tribes, soused to the gills, gathered together to witness a cracking match...'

'Having had the pleasure of getting to know both families here today, I can see that this occasion is going to be a great opportunity for two wonderful sets of people to meet and mingle.'

'A wedding is a wonderful opportunity for people to make new friends and form relationships. So as chief bridesmaid can I just say: "Bagsy first dance with the best man"!'

'This occasion reminds me of my own wedding, all those years ago. And what a close-run thing *that* was!'

End on a high!
Nobody wants your speech to end. So leave them wanting more with something like…

'I'd like to thank you for your patience and kind attention, and to those of you who managed to stay awake: cheers!'

'That's all from me, except to say that, for those of you who've never given a speech at a wedding before, if you get an audience half as generous as you lot, you'll enjoy every minute of it…'

'So, without further ado, I'd like you charge your glass and thank the Almighty that I'm finally going to sit down and shut up. Cheers!'

'To the happy couple, may their happiness be complete, their marriage long and prosperous and every wedding speech they hear be funnier and shorter than mine…'

'And, in the words of that world-famous orator, Bugs Bunny: "That's all, folks"!'

Final thoughts

'One final thought. If marriage is a two-way street, how come my wife keeps telling me that it's "my way or the highway"?'

'One final thought. Always listen carefully to your partner's advice, so that when things go wrong you can say "I told you so"!'

'And finally, marriage should be like supporting a football team: sometimes happy, sometimes sad, but always exciting for about an hour and a half on a Saturday!

'Don't forget. Never put off until tomorrow something you can do today – especially if that something is saying "I love you".'

'Finally, having you all here today reminds Jeremy and me of just how much love there is in the world. And now that we're married, we intend to make a whole lot more…'

Toasts

'For richer, for poorer, in sickness and in health…
Pray charge your glasses and toast our delightful newly-weds,
Jane and John!'

'Now let's all stand, fill our glasses, and wish today's happy
couple: Love, Laughter and Long Life!'

'Today, Irene and Tony have made the most solemn
commitment possible between two people. And so on this
joyous day we raise our glasses to… the bride and groom!'

'Ladies and gentlemen, boys and girls… Please be upstanding
and raise your glasses to… the adorable couple!'

Prayers

'We give thanks for this special day, and ask for God's blessing to shine upon Graham and Georgina, whose wedding we have been privileged to witness. Watch over them and guide them as they embark on their new life together, and grant them the strength to cope with life's highs and lows along the way.'

'May your marriage be blessed with God's love, and be a shining example to all of the virtues of love, compassion, tolerance and fellowship…'

(Said by husband or wife:)
'Lord, grant us, as husband and wife, a true understanding and love for one another. Fill us with faith and trust, and grant us the grace to live together in peace and harmony. May we always bear with one another's weaknesses and grow from each other's strengths.'

(Said by husband or wife:)
'Lord, may the love that has brought us together here today grow and mature with each passing year, and may all around us share in the love we bring to each other. Bring us ever closer to You through our love for each other. Amen.'

'God, bless all our family and friends who have joined us here to share in our special day. Bind us together in your love, and give us all the kindness and patience and wisdom to support each other in all we do. May we rejoice in your blessings for all our days. Amen.'

Sample speeches

Usually it's easiest to build a speech bit by bit.
This is what this section is for. It's full of material that
you can pinch and use as is, or adapt to suit your own
needs and ideas.

You may already have decided on a beginning, middle
and end for your speech, using the previous section.
The following pages should help you fill out the rest.
Remember, it's always worth timing your speech. It
may look short written down, but take ages to get
through when you leave in time for laughs!

About the bride: She's one in a million

Father of the bride

'My little girl is one in a million. She's beautiful, like a never-ending summer's day. She's got the patience of a saint. She's intelligent, funny and has an amazing grasp of current affairs and politics. She can cook like Nigella Lawson, play golf like Nick Faldo and dance like Darcey Bussell.'

'Rob, I can say with my hand on my heart that you're one of the luckiest men alive. [To be said aside to groom] And she writes a cracking Father of the Bride speech as well...'

'Anyone who knows my daughter – and I assume that's all of you here, unless you're gate-crashing (in which case, pay attention) – knows that she is quite simply, one in a million. Which by my reckoning means there's only another 20 or so like her in the country. So, any single lads out there, I'd get your skates on, get out there and try and track one down for yourself!'

'I think you'll all agree that Lisa – my little girl – is one in a million. She certainly is to my wife and me, and I know Tim thinks so too. She's always been a daughter to be proud of – but, more than that, she's a great inspiration to everyone around her. My wife Helen and I are both immensely proud of her.'

Groom

'A friend of mine asked me about Lisa the other day and I tried to explain to him all the qualities I love about her – her intelligence, her humour, her beauty, her sense of fun, her loyalty. "She must be one in a million", he said. I thought about it for a moment and then replied, "Not one in a million, mate. She's just The One"…'

'I thank my lucky stars that I found Patricia. In fact, I think of myself as one of the luckiest men who ever lived. I just wish some of that luck would rub off when I'm picking my lottery tickets. Although, if the truth were known, I feel like I've hit the jackpot already. There's no bonus ball I'm afraid though, darling…'

'I was trying to rank myself in terms of the luckiest men that ever lived the other day. I thought of the man who won the lottery on successive weekends. I considered Bobby Moore – playing for the Hammers AND skippering a World Cup-winning team. Or Kylie's personal trainer. But then I realized that I must be the luckiest man EVER. Why? Because Lisa is one in a million…'

Best man

'David, as your best man I have to congratulate you on managing to land a complete stunner like Nicole. She's absolutely beautiful, she's funny, she's intelligent and if she can cope with your unhealthy obsession with Torquay United, she really must be one in a million.'

'Ever since Jack and I met at primary school and he fell in love with one of the dinner ladies, I've wondered what type of woman he'd end up with. So I was bowled over when he met the gorgeous girl he married today. She really is one in a million and I'm delighted for them both. I've got just one question, Jack. How did you manage it?'

'Roy has proved himself to be a real, true friend over the years – in that respect, he's a man in a million. And he's met his match in Kerry, because anyone can see that she's a woman in a million too. Congratulations to you both.'

Chief bridesmaid

'Today I've been doing my duty as chief bridesmaid – and it's been great fun. But for years, Laura has been doing her duty as best friend. She's comforted me when I've been sobbing my eyes out over various losers, she's congratulated me when I've been promoted. We've shopped till we've dropped together, shared tonnes of chocolate and what must have been hundreds of bottles of wine. In all that time, Laura has been unfailingly kind, funny, generous and altogether one in a million. Tom, I'm sure you know it already, but let me say it again. You are a very, very lucky man.'

About the bride: Daddy's girl

Father of the bride

'Katie was the kind of child any father would be proud of. She excelled in music, was popular at school, was respectful to her seniors and protective of those younger than her. Darling... [turns to the mother of the bride] are you sure she's mine?'

'When Emma was born, I shed a tear or two for my beautiful new daughter. On her first day at school, I think I cried more than her. And when she showed me her GCSE results, I was inconsolable with happiness.'

'Sarah was always a tomboy. I think her first words were "Manchester United". As a child, she was never happier than when she was climbing a tree or heading a ball. I can hardly believe that the vision of loveliness before me today is my daughter. You'll never manage a decent goal kick in that frock though, love.'

'The house has seemed very quiet since Karen left home. You can barely hear anything but the sound of my wallet sighing with relief.'

Groom

'Penny is her father's daughter in so many ways. She's smart, she's astute, she's intelligent, she's generous and, funnily enough, *she's always right too.*'

'Harry is a Super-Dad as far as Charlotte is concerned – and he is equally devoted to her. When he walked her down the aisle today, I know that he was bursting with pride but I'm also sure that he must have felt some trepidation at the thought of giving away his little girl. So let me take this opportunity to assure my new father-in-law that Charlotte is as precious to me as she is to him.'

'I have to admit that I was a bit nervous about meeting Holly's father as I knew that he was very protective about his only daughter. But once he'd sent the boys round to my place to straighten out a few things, we got on just fine. Er, didn't we, Mr Ross, sir?'

Best man

'All of us who know Mr Stephens will be aware that he is a formidable character as well as a devoted father. He and Miranda are very close and, not surprisingly, given his strength, his generosity and his wisdom, she's always looked up to her dad. It would take quite a man to live up to him, but in Hal, Miranda has found that man.'

'Tom has told me that, when the time comes, he hopes he can be as good a father as his new father-in-law.'

'When I knew I was going to be best man, Helena's dad gave me a piece of advice to pass on to the groom. He told me that, however bad the situation, there are some magic words Sean can say to Helena that are guaranteed to make everything all right again. So here they are Sean, repeat after me: "Can I make you some fish-finger sarnies, love"?'

Chief bridesmaid
'When we were growing up, Mr Robinson was always everyone's favourite dad. We all looked up to him, especially Hannah. I want to take this opportunity, Mr Robinson, to say "thank you" for your hospitality. Hannah is a wonderful girl. She's a good friend, a fine colleague and she's going to be a great wife. I'm sure she'd agree that all these things are a credit to you.'

'Sarah's dad is truly a man of many talents. In fact, during the time I've known him, he's been Sarah's chauffeur, banker, agony aunt, secretary, and occasionally personal shopper. I'm sure that now Sarah and John are married he's looking forward to a peaceful retirement.'

'Georgia and her dad have always been close, and Max has been a tower of strength in the run up to the wedding. Never has a man endured so many conversations about flowers, veils, shoes, dresses and canapés. And all this without falling asleep once.'

About the bride: My daughter/sister/wife

Father of the bride

'They say that your own wedding is the best day of your life and ours was certainly wonderful. But I think my wife would agree that the wedding day of our lovely daughter has been even better. It's just marvellous to see her so happy. Take my word for it – being the father of the bride is great. I think I'd better stop eating and drinking before I burst with pride.'

'Elizabeth has always had a reputation for being rather choosy. Only the best would do when it came to clothes, hairstyles and cars – and believe me, she's given me a few grey hairs in my time. But I'm certainly glad she was choosy in her choice of groom. Paul is a man to gladden any father-in-law's heart, and I know he'll make my daughter happy.'

'Whatever people might say, it's not all sugar and spice and all things nice with daughters. In fact, Laura has brought home her fair share of slugs and snails, but she's always given us so much joy and never more so than today. She's found the right man and we couldn't be happier for them both.'

Groom

'The first time I saw Hannah I was dazzled by her. If you had told me then that we would one day be married, I wouldn't have believed you – although I would have wanted to. I can honestly say that I don't think anyone could be as happy as I am today. I'm immensely proud to be able to call her my wife.'

'They say that it's not possible to love someone you can't laugh with. Well, I can certainly laugh with Lucy, although I must admit she seemed to be losing her sense of humour in the days leading up to the wedding. I wouldn't say she was anxious, but she made the vicar rehearse his part of the service five times.'

'Brides are always supposed to look radiant, but Pamela really does. I just keep looking at her and feeling that I can't believe my luck.'

'I suppose you'll be expecting a few laughs in this speech. But I know I need to tread carefully. I don't want to upset my in-laws and hear my wife going round and introducing me to everyone as her "first husband".'

Brother of the bride/best man

'My sister was an assertive kind of child. On many occasions, as I counted my bruises, I found myself wondering what kind of man she'd marry. Well, today I've got the answer. My new brother-in-law Steve, is intelligent, witty, generous – and very, very brave.'

'Of course, there are a lot of things I could tell you about my little sister. But I won't, mainly because of the hefty bribe she promised me before I started preparing this speech. [Turns to groom:] You didn't know I was coming to the Maldives with you, did you?'

'I couldn't have wished for my lovely sister to marry a better guy. They truly are a very lucky couple.'

Sister of the bride/Chief bridesmaid

'As Marianne's younger sister, I have some advice for the groom. Peter, always treat Marianne gently and with respect. Never forget to listen to her opinions and value her contribution to your marriage. Never forget that she hates milk in her coffee, that she loves roses and can't stand classical music. And above all – and I speak from bitter experience – never, ever borrow her mascara without asking.'

'I think that perhaps because I'm Emily's big sister, I sometimes worry about her. But not today. Emily has definitely found the right man in Edward and I'm happy and proud to be their chief bridesmaid.'

'Ever since she was small, my sister Stella has had a reputation for being just a teeny bit fussy about her clothes. As the chief bridesmaid who helped her get ready this morning, all I can say on the subject is that I need a drink – and I need it now!'

About the bride: She wears the trousers

Father of the bride

'It will come as no surprise to you, Adam, that Carina was nicknamed "Miss Bossy Boots" at school. Looking back, I suppose she was displaying her leadership abilities even then. She certainly led my wife and me up the garden path many a time!'

'Jo was always strong-willed. Even as a child, if there was something she wanted, she didn't stop until she got it. So, Nigel, I guess you didn't stand a chance. But then again, where would Nigel be without someone there to run his life for him?'

'Tomboy she used to be, lady she is now. But don't be fooled by that beautiful smile. Sara is a formidable opponent. Woe betide anyone who disagrees with her. Ladies and gentlemen, I'm afraid you'll have to forgive me for the following gap in my speech – Sara edited the next bit out and I'm under strict instructions not to mention... er, sorry, that's been crossed out too.'

Groom

'My wife wears the trousers. Beautifully. And as you can see, she looks great in a dress too.'

'Because Anita has such a successful career, people assume that she wears the trousers in our household. Actually, I do – she just makes sure they're Armani.'

'I should have realized the first time I met Karen what I was letting myself in for. Not only did she insist that she bought the drinks, she drove me home, told me I was to phone her, told me when to phone her, then gave me a full account of what she expected me to say when I did phone her. Well, I've always enjoyed a bit of domination!'

'I used to be disorganized. Those of you who visited my student digs will know just how disorganized. Who can forget the smell of wet socks drying under the grill? I'm pleased to say all that changed the day Tracey moved in. She might wear the trousers, but at least I get to wear clean, dry socks.'

'Some people call my wife "bossy". I call her "ma'am". No, seriously – I call her strong and independent, and am honoured to have her as my companion.'

Best man

'We all know she's a, *ahem*, strong character, but boy are we pleased Jess has taken John in hand. Let's face it, John, it's a brave woman who can solve your wardrobe dilemmas. Even the moths wouldn't touch your suits in the old days. But look at you now. Okay, you've spilt the soup down your shirt and your flies are undone (only kidding), but I almost fancy you myself these days.'

Chief bridesmaid

'I first met Clare when we both joined the Brownies at the age of six, and I can honestly say she is the bossiest person I've ever had the pleasure of knowing. How many girls aged seven would insist they knew better than Brown Owl how to light a fire? She proved it later, of course, when she managed to set fire to the chemistry labs.'

'Who else could the school have chosen to be head girl? Frankly, Jane was acting like head girl from the moment she set foot in in the door. The teachers didn't stand a chance – they couldn't get a word in edgeways. I must say I think Harry is coping remarkably well. YOU CAN TAKE THE EARPLUGS OUT NOW, HARRY.'

About the bride: She's a great mum

Father of the bride
'Not only is my daughter Lisa going to make Tim a fantastic wife, we already know what a great mother she is. And I know that her daughter Alice is looking forward to becoming a step-sister just as soon as she gets the chance!'

'When Kate brought Paul to meet us we also fell in love. Not with him, of course, but with his daughter Annie... and we know Kate feels the same way and is going to do everything she can to be a great step-mum...'

'Many couples say that their wedding day is the best day of their lives. But not Bella and Andy. That day happened six months ago when their son George was born. And as for George, every day is the best day of his life, because he has a great dad and the most wonderful mother in the world!'

Groom
'Now, everyone knows that for Lisa, this marriage involves taking on a big kid. The mess, the broken nights, the temper tantrums... and as well as looking after me, she'll become step-mum to my son Danny!'

'Emma is not the only girl I suggested marriage to this year... I also asked her daughter Hayley! Frankly, asking a father for their daughter's hand in marriage is nothing compared to asking a toddler. However, once she knew that I loved the Tweenies and McDonalds, she gave us her blessing.'

'As everybody knows, Anna has another man in her life. Her son, Alfie. And if she is half as good a wife as she is a mother, I'm the luckiest man on earth.'

'Today, is not just about Ellie and me. It's about us AND our kids becoming one big happy family. And I know that Ellie will be as great a step-mum as she is a mum.'

Best man
'I can reveal a great secret to you today. I know what made Lewis fall in love with Nicki. It wasn't her gorgeous good looks, her kind nature, or her fantastic pay packet. No, it was the day he caught her playing football with her son Louis. When someone is that great a mother, you just know they'll be a wonderful wife.'

'The groom Ben is NOT the luckiest man in the world today to be marrying Eva. No, that honour goes to his son, David, who from this day forth gets unlimited access to Eva's home cooking and comes home to Eva a good three hours before Ben does!'

'They say, "Never work with children or animals." But I guess Jo wasn't listening. Today she becomes the official and much-loved step-mum to two children, a dog, a parrot, a gerbil and a goldfish called Britney!'

'I know that Isabelle must really love Charlie because only the best has ever been good enough for her kids!'

About the bride: She's expecting

Father of the bride

'As you must all know by now, Joanna is expecting. And did anyone ever see a more beautiful, blooming bride walk up the aisle? I speak for all my family when I say how proud we are of her.'

'When Sarah told us she was getting married to Tony, my wife and I couldn't have been more delighted. We rushed out to buy champagne and celebrate. A month later they were back for Sunday lunch saying they had something serious to tell us. We held our breath for a minute, I can tell you. Was the wedding off, we wondered? What on earth did they want to tell us? Well, ladies and gentlemen, I can now tell you. Sarah is expecting our first grandchild, and we couldn't be happier for them. So please be upstanding and drink a toast to Sarah, Tony and the bump!'

Groom

'Ladies and gents, those of you who know me will not be surprised to learn that when Caroline told me we were expecting a baby, my reaction wasn't quite textbook stuff. Champagne, flowers and kisses, I believe, are standard. I, on the other hand, just stood there open-mouthed, wondering how on earth it had happened! But as the truth sank in, we realized that we that we could not have been happier. So please join us in a toast to our imminent arrival.

'For years, ladies and gentlemen, friends and family have told me that it really was time for me to settle down. And for years I have completely ignored them. But being with Karen has made me stop and think about my priorities in life.
I know now that I want my life to be centred around her and our family. And, yes, it's already started – we're expecting our first child next April…'

Bride

'When Anthony and I decided to get married, it was because we realized that the time had come to cement our relationship and start work on making a family together. When he proposed and I accepted, "overjoyed" is not an adequate description of how we both felt. So much so, in fact, that our celebrations have resulted in our plans being brought forward quite substantially. So everyone please mark April 26 in your diaries now, as that is the date that we are expecting our first baby!'

Best man

'Biology was never Giles' best subject when we were at school. So when he and Juliet told me they were expecting, it came as something of a surprise that Giles had finally worked out what to do. Several orange juices later (yes, they've given up alcohol together!), the mystery was solved – it turns out Juliet took A' level biology.'

About the groom: When he was a kid

Father of the bride

'I've heard that John was a precocious child. He walked and talked before he was one; he could read and write by the time he was four, and could forge his parents' signature by the time he was eight!'

'Malcolm, the groom's father, has been regaling me with stories about Jim's childhood, and I feel it would be rude of me not to share one of them with you today. Apparently Jim was the primary school Romeo. Not that you'd believe it today, but I'm told that he used his "special powers" to get the girls to kiss him. From what Claire's told me about his dubious chat-up routine, it sounds like he abandoned his "special powers" in favour of "Special Brew"...'

'Given that Lucy and George grew up together, I'm in the rare position of having known my new son-in-law since he was a babe in arms. And what a babe he was! I'm not saying he was ugly, but why else would his granny have knitted all those blue full-face balaclavas?'

Best man

'Nick and I have been friends since primary school. I think we bonded on our first day because we were the only two kids in the playground who spoke Klingon. I even thought he'd come in character, but I now see those ears are hereditary. Sorry, Mr Johnston.'

'Tony and I spent all our school holidays together when we were kids. If I wasn't round his house, he was round mine. We always pretended we were the latest action heroes. When I was the Six Million Dollar Man, he was Wonder Woman. When I was Batman he was Catwoman. He was Lois Lane to my Superman. And as I'm sure he'll prove to you all later, he can still cut a dash in tights.'

'When Jerry was a kid, he wasn't much to look at. Crazy as it may sound today, when he was a boy he could break mirrors just by looking in them. I don't know who cut his hair back then, but whoever it was obviously had a grudge. But miracles do happen and, as you can see, time (not to mention a great deal of expensive cosmetic surgery) has turned our ugly duckling into a swan.'

'Craig and I were always getting into trouble when we were young. Actually, let me rephrase that. *I* was always getting in to trouble while Craig would get away with blue murder. He's always been able to charm his way out of a mess and often ended up with an apology from his victims. So what was the little artful dodger's secret? Perhaps his father – an estate agent – could explain.'

'Dan was a real mummy's boy when we were kids. He'd get the best packed lunches in school, he'd be driven to and from school every day and was put to bed at the merest hint of a cold. But as you can see, he's no less of a man for it. OK, so he's no Charles Atlas... and he's a bit of a hypochondriac... and he can't cook... er, and he's never done his own washing... but he is a demon flower-arranger.'

Bride

'I grew up in the same street as Robbie so I've known him since we were about eight. In fact, my friends and I used to keep scores on who we thought were the most fanciable boys in the street. Even then Robbie got the highest marks. Maybe it was his Marc Bolan perm, or his wispy moustache, or the way he could burn rubber on his moped. Or maybe it was because he was the only boy over ten in our street.'

'When we were kids, Richard refused to speak to me – or any other girls for that matter. He only liked cowboys and Indians, and builders, and motorbikes and the police and the army. Well, it was good enough for the Village People, so who am I to judge?'

'Mark's sister has been kind enough to share some of his childhood photos with me. His first potty training accident... his school sports day... his FIRST GIRLFRIEND! Now you know I'm not the jealous type but... She's blonde, she's cute, she's got a great smile, she's obviously mad about him and you can tell from the way she wore her nappy that the kid had style.'

Chief bridesmaid

'Lucy and I first met Simon at playschool. She was the only girl he'd allow in the Wendy house and he was the only boy she'd allow to play with her on the water table. It was obviously love at first sight.'

'Suzie, Mike and I all went to the same school which means I've had the dubious pleasure of seeing Mike in a cagoule. He was the sort of kid other boys looked up to. Whether it was his multi-function utility belt or his animal-print desert boots that first caught Suzie's eye, I've yet to be told.'

About the groom: My brother/son

Groom's brother/best man

'As Jack's elder brother, I've always felt quite protective of him. So when he told me he'd met the most wonderful woman in the world, I felt it was my duty to check her out. No, not like that! The problem is, I'm a lager man whereas Jack drinks bitter. I'm a rugby fan, he's a football man. I ski, he hates the cold. I'm an owl, he's a lark. It's not often we can agree on the same thing. But with my new sister-in-law, Tilly, I can only say, there's an exception to every rule.'

'As the great Vinnie Jones would say, today's been… "emotional". Standing here, on my brother's wedding day, in the company of so many friends and family, I feel overwhelmed by an unusual sense of affection towards Pete. I've realized today that the insignificant little twerp I've grown up with is actually a much-loved, much-respected man who thoroughly deserves the love and attention that Olivia has been kind enough to offer him.'

'As David's twin, I have lived my life alongside his. It's as though we've been running the same race together. But today, it's time for me to hand over my baton to Amanda. I wish you both all the luck and love in the world as you run life's course together. As with all great sporting partnerships, when one is weak, the other will be strong, and whatever hurdles are put in your way, you'll get over them together. Enjoy your journey.'

'I've learnt to be wary about Carl's opinions. It was, after all, he who convinced me I'd look good with a moustache, told me cerise was the new black and persuaded me to swap my open-top MG for his Ford Fiesta. But when he told me that Sarah was the best thing that had ever happened to him, there was no question – for once he'd got it absolutely right.'

Groom's sister/chief bridesmaid

'As you probably all know, the groom is, in fact, my brother. Quite what attracted Sara to my childhood tormentor I'll never know. All I can say is if her ideal man burps, farts, swears, smells and snores, then she's found Mr Right.'

'When Polly first started going out with my brother, I had mixed emotions. Here was my best friend, the person with whom I'd laughed, cried, shared secrets, watched soppy movies, shopped till we dropped and eaten copious amounts of chocolate with. And he was mad about Polly!'

'I don't feel that I'm losing a brother, any more than I feel I'm losing my best friend. The fact that two of the most valuable people in my life have fallen in love just fills me with great joy. Knowing them as well as I do, I'm confident that their love will only grow and flourish further as the years go by.'

About the groom: He's mad about...

Father of the bride

'When I found out that Luke had a first-class degree from Oxford, I was naturally quite pleased. When Sophie told me that he had been tipped for the board I was pleasantly surprised. But when she told me he was a Bolton Wanderers season-ticket holder I went ballistic!'

'Apparently, Steve's a bit of a gadget freak. If it's small, slim and gives you non-stop information 24/7, he's got to have it. And now I come to think of it, I can see exactly what attracted him to Lizzie.'

'Andrew, like me, is mad about motorsport. We've bonded over team victories, fallen out over our Top Ten Drivers of All Time lists, and shared tears when Murray Walker retired. So when Andy was setting a wedding date, he checked with me first that the big day didn't clash with a race day. But I'd just like to say to those cynics out there who've noticed that their honeymoon is in Monte Carlo – where I'll be joining them for day or two – that this is pure coincidence.'

Best man

'Nathan and I became friends when we met at scout camp aged 10. Ever since then, he's been mad about the great outdoors. In fact, he fancies himself as a bit of a Ray Mears character. He can make a shower out of a pair of trousers, a tent out of a parachute and knows how to stun a grizzly bear with a frisbee. But ask him to make you a simple cup of tea...'

'Bill and I worked together in a rock 'n' roll record shop when we were at university. Since then it's been Elvis this, Elvis that. So when it came to choosing the song to be played for the couple's first dance, it was obviously going to be a tough choice. Fortunately, I got a sneak preview of his shortlist this afternoon and hastily withdrew "Hard-headed Woman", "Crying in the Chapel"... and "You're the Devil in Disguise".'

'It can't have escaped anyone's notice that Rick is mad about Arsenal – a love he, unfortunately, has not been able to share with Marie. So what advice can I give to Marie, the soon-to-be football widow? One: if you want a favour doing, ask just before kick-off, but tell him it can be done after the match. He'll be putty in your hands. Two: tell him you understand the offside rule. It doesn't matter if you don't, it'll just save you hours of tedious explanations with ketchup bottle and pepper-pots. And three: go out shopping on Saturdays.'

Bride

'When I was first introduced to Barry, I was told that he loved cooking. As someone who has to refer to Delia to boil an egg, I knew I had to have him. I imagined breakfasts in bed, candlelit dinners and romantic picnics, all created by the love of my life. What more could a girl want? Unfortunately, what his mates failed to tell me is that it's not so much cooking he's mad about, but stuffing his face and swooning over Nigella Lawson!'

'I'll admit I had some ulterior motives when I first met Joe. It wasn't his gorgeous blue eyes that attracted me. Nor his rugged handsomeness. I'll confess it was his Workmate (his Black & Decker Workmate, not his colleague, I hasten to add!). The thing is, I needed some shelves doing and he looked keen, willing and able. OK, so the house is now immaculate, but his hands are like sandpaper, he's always putting his back out and he's developed an allergy to paint stripper. Roll on the honeymoon!'

Chief bridesmaid

'I remember when Mandy came back from her first date with Darren. She had stars in her eyes and was walking on cloud nine. She told me all about his puppy-dog eyes, his steadfast loyalty, his shiny hair and his irrepressible energy. It was ages before I realized she was describing his beloved German Shepherd, Benjy.'

About the groom: He's not squeaky clean

Father of the bride

'When I was first introduced to Jim I thought he was a fine, upstanding man. He treated me with respect, did the whole down-on-one-knee thing, bought me a fine bottle of vintage claret and told me how much he adored my daughter. What a gentleman... or so I thought! It turns out that he'd downloaded a "How to suck up to your future father-in-law" checklist from the Internet. I only know this because I came across it whilst searching for a "How to make your future son-in-law squirm!" list.'

'Much to Jeremy's embarrassment, I've been talking to his mother. We've spent ages comparing notes on our respective offspring and now both sets of parents feel much better informed! Apparently squeaky-clean Jeremy wasn't always such a smooth-talking, sharp-suited, go-getter. In fact, I believe his first suit was bought for his first court appearance.'

'When Nick invited Claire's mother and me over to a dinner that he'd cooked, we thought she'd landed herself a New Man. What we didn't know was that he'd defrosted a pie Claire had made previously and just garnished it with a sprig of parsley.'

Best man

'Ben has always been an entrepreneur. But at school the teachers didn't really respect his commercial spirit. While he considered his money-making enterprises demonstrated creative thinking and immense initiative, his suspension certificate chose to describe it as "extortion".'

'Matt is a man with a past. He's been there, done that, worn the T-shirt. His philosophy has always been: try everything once, and if you enjoy it, try it again. He's flirted with the law (and a few WPCs when necessary); he's broken a few hearts and he's caused a few blushes. But at the end of the day, he'd lay his life on the line for the people he loves. He's been a true friend to me for 20 years, and I know he'll be the most loyal, devoted husband to Mandy for the rest of their lives.'

'My friendship with Simon dates back to our first day at secondary school. I was immediately drawn to him because he looked like the cool one. I'm not sure if it was his bleached blonde hair or his skin-tight trousers that made him stand out from the crowd, or his huge badge collection and his Masters of the Universe backpack. Man, that boy had style! Best of all, his attitude earned the reputation of school rebel. He refused to wear black socks. He did his homework in biro. And once he even cracked a test tube on purpose. He was wild!'

'As we all know, Chris is a highly successful businessman now. But that hasn't always been the case. In fact his early forays into employment were a disaster. He was fired from his paper round when his boss found out he'd used the papers to make a life-size papier mâché dinosaur for a school project. He got a verbal warning from the landlord of the Dog and Duck for downing a yard of ale every time a customer said to him "have one for yourself". And his milk round came to an abrupt halt when he was arrested for float rage.'

'Life hasn't always been a bed of roses for Charles and Kate. Although you might think butter wouldn't melt in his mouth, he's had to do a fair bit of grovelling to get to where he is today. On their first date Charles got so drunk that, at the end of the night, he gave £20 to Kate and his phone number to the cab driver.'

Chief bridesmaid
'Tanya always said that she liked a bit of rough, but nothing prepared me for the first time I met Joe. He'd just got back from work on the building site and was covered, head to toe, in muck. His hair was stuck on end, his face was covered in dust, his clothes were caked in mud and his hands were blackened with grease. This was going to be difficult. How could I possibly pretend to her that this oil slick in front of me was an Adonis? But when he started talking, it all fitted into place. His charm, his humour, his compassion and his generous spirit shone through. And as you can all see today, he's not bad looking when he scrubs up, either.'

About the groom: He's a couch potato

Father of the bride

'I'd always imagined my daughter marrying a high-flying, thrusting executive who'd spend his working week flying around the world. But that's not exactly how you'd sum up Brian. Now there are plenty of jobs where you're forced to sit down all day, but most of them involve a desk and an office. However Brian tells me that I'm still stuck in the twentieth century – that real men now work from home, from their sofa. I'm not sure whether I'm behind the times, or he's a complete layabout. That said, at least he's always there for Sophie when she gets back from work – even if he is watching *Neighbours*!'

'I'm not saying my son-in-law's lazy, but he sent one of his friends to ask me for my daughter's hand in marriage. So I exacted my revenge by sending my response in an enormous box – thereby obliging Matt to get off his behind and go and collect it from the post office depot!'

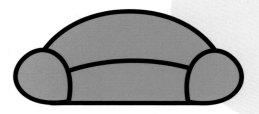

Best man

'Now I'm not one to cast aspersions on anyone, but as you might have noticed in church today, "energetic" is not Mark's middle name. You could even go as far as saying that he's a hot contender for The World's Laziest Man title. But to give him his due, when it comes to women he's put in a lot of chasing, despite being given the run around so often. But with Fiona it's been a different story. He'd jump through hoops for her, he'd run a million miles for one of her smiles, gets a spring in his step at the mention of her name and turned cartwheels when she agreed to marry him.'

'Richard is so lazy that he'll only buy stuff for his home if it comes with a remote control. If it can't be switched on and switched off at the touch of a keypad he doesn't want to know. So when Zoe whispered in his ear that she really wanted him to turn her on, he promised her he knew all the right buttons. And the rest, as they say, is history.'

'Ed has always been a couch potato. At university he was even known as King Edward. It takes a lot to get him moving – especially if *Animal Hospital* is on TV – and you could end up waiting for years for him to get ready to go out. So I think we should acknowledge the effort that he's made in being here today by raising a glass. Don't worry Ed, you can stay seated!'

Bride

'I think it's fair to say that John and I were drawn together by our mutual laziness. We both like nothing more than pizza and a bottle of wine in front of the telly, and the thought of spending hours getting dressed up just so we can go and meet a few mates seems like a complete waste of time. So we hope you all appreciate the effort we've gone to today…'

'Despite Alan being the love of my life, there's no denying that he's bone idle, which is why I had no idea that he was planning to propose. When he said he had something to ask me, I thought it would be whether I would make him a cup of tea.'

Chief bridesmaid

'I remember how excited Kelly was when Chris asked her to marry him. She came over to my house and couldn't stop gushing over her ring, her fiancé and the wonderful life they were going to share together. I, for my part, was as astonished as Kelly was excited. Knowing how lazy Chris is, and how difficult he finds moving his backside off the sofa, I did wonder how he managed to summon up the energy to reach into his back pocket, pull out the ring, get down on one knee, and still find breath to propose. No wonder they need a break in the sun.'

'Contrary to popular belief, Hugh doesn't suffer from narcolepsy. I've checked with his parents and I'm pleased to confirm that he's just bone idle.'

About the groom: He's going places

Father of the bride

'I just wanted to say a few words about how proud I am of my new son-in-law, Jake. During the course of his engagement to Julia, I've come to realize that he's a dedicated and diligent man, who's prepared to work hard to achieve his goals. His efforts have now paid off and he's won the ultimate accolade, my daughter.'

'When Andrea said she'd met the man she wanted to marry, I was extremely curious to know what he did. Then she said he was "self-employed", and my heart sank as I envisioned a layabout whose afternoons were divided between the bookies and the pub. Of course, it turns out that Dominic actually runs his own successful business, and if he works as hard at his marriage as he does at his job, I'll see you all at their silver wedding anniversary…'

Best man

'When Matt and I were at school, he was always going places – the moon was a favourite, to the top of the class was another, and who could forget his plan to dance on stage with Michael Jackson? He's certainly never lacked ambition, which is why I knew that once he'd set his sights on Kimberley, he wouldn't rest until she was his.'

'I remember when James told me he was going to build his own home. Typical, I thought, he couldn't find the house he wanted on the market, so he decided to make his own from scratch. That's the thing about James, he's always been a bit of a go-getter. Sadly, it's rarely to the bar to buy anyone a drink.'

'As many of you know, Jack and I were at university together. We even read the same subject. Sadly, that's where the similarity ends. He's going places. I'm not. So Sasha, count yourself lucky you ended up being chatted up by him and not me at that fateful first meeting. Otherwise you could have been heading for Clacton, not the Caribbean, for your honeymoon.'

'Since he first met Rochelle, David has really started to go places. It was "to hell" when he first asked her out, "on your bike" when he tried to coax her into the bedroom, "to the hairdressers" when he first met her parents – and, of course, when he proposed… to the most expensive jewellers in town.'

'There's only been one occasion in the history of my friendship with Henry when his self-confidence has taken a dive. During a game of conkers, a particularly energetic swing from me accidentally took his two front teeth out. Poor old Henry was beside himself, thinking that people would forever more be shouting "Mind the gap!" and laughing in his face. Ultimately, I managed to convince him that he could still lead a normal life despite his impediment, and he picked himself up, dusted himself down and soon reverted back into the precocious little so-and-so we all know and love. Little did I realize then just how well Henry would bounce back, managing to get his teeth into someone as ravishing as Lucinda.'

'When Bob and I were little, I lost count of the number of times a grown-up remarked, "He's going places, that Robert." Secretly jealous, I used to laugh to myself that the only place Robert was likely to go was jail. But adolescent rivalry aside, I can see that the adults were right (as always) and Bob has indeed done very well for himself. There's the fantastic job, his unique physique, his world-beating collection of beer mats, and now of course, his perfect wife.'

Bride
'When Dave and I first started going out with each other, I was attracted by his ambition, drive and dynamism. I fancied him because he knew what he wanted, and he wasn't afraid to go for it – which probably explains why he's been so successful in his career. When he proposed to me, I realized that without those qualities our marriage would still be as strong, and I'd love him just as much. Today I swore that I'd love and respect him, whether he's at the top of his tree – or completely out of it.'

Chief bridesmaid
'When Charlotte told me that she'd agreed to marry Will, I have to admit to feeling an overwhelming sense of loss. Who was going to sit drinking white wine with me, lamenting the

lack of decent men in the world? My despair didn't last too long, though, when I realized what a catch Will is. He's great-looking, brilliantly funny and has a promising career that'll help keep Charlotte in the manner to which she'd like to become accustomed. In fact, it's more than fair to say that our groom is really going places. OK, that's enough sucking up from me. Will: when are you going to introduce me to one of your friends from work?'

About the families: Heartfelt thanks

Father of the bride

'When my daughter told us she was getting married, she said: "Don't worry, George and I will organize everything." And we thought, 'Yeah, right!' We had visions of sitting down to eat the one thing Anna can actually cook – cheese on toast. But today has made me more proud than ever of my little girl... so thank you, Anna and George, for an elegant, wonderful occasion!'

'My daughter is, as you know, somewhat independently minded. In fact, she and Eddie have insisted on paying for today themselves. Obviously, my wife and I offered, but would they accept our help? No! Eventually, they agreed we could pay for one thing... this ornamental cake knife... [Picks up the item and looks at it]. I must say, you don't get much for five grand these days! Seriously, though, they did do it all themselves – and hasn't it been wonderful?'

'I think there comes a time in any father's life when he has to accept that he doesn't have all the answers. But that's OK. Because his wife does! I think we'd all agree she has done us proud today...'

Groom

'They say that love is the greatest teacher. So I'd like to thank my new wife for everything she's taught me over the last few months. That serviettes are actually manufactured in *sixty-two* different shades of pink. That the wrong wedding cake is a choice you live with for the rest of your life, and that my signature looks like a five year-old's! Seriously, if my wife hadn't eaten, slept and drunk this wedding for the last year, we wouldn't all be having the fantastic time we are today. So thank you from the bottom of my heart, Emma.'

'This wedding would have been nothing without the superb negotiating skills of Helen's mother. If there was a deal to be done, she did it. If there was a difference of opinion, she settled it. In fact I believe she's being seconded to the UN as soon as this reception is over. And [turning to the mother of the bride] I was wondering if perhaps, Mrs Phillips, since we've bonded over the organization of the wedding and are now related, I can finally drop the 'Mrs Phillips' and call you something that truly reflects our new relationship... Ma'am!'

Best man

'I heard about a man in America who claimed to have attended more weddings than anyone else in the world. Nearly 30,000! He says the key to a good wedding is: good seating, good eating and good friends. And what fantastic chairs they are... No, really, I would add to that list: good hosts. And let's face it, in Gemma's parents, Roger and Anne, we have the very best...'

'In Roman times, after a sumptuous feast, the revellers would show their appreciation to their hosts by vomiting. So, just to say, Mr and Mrs Smith, if you should see any of that happening later, it's simply a well-deserved compliment!'

'I wanted to thank Emily's family, firstly for inviting us all here today and treating us all to this fabulous reception, and secondly for allowing Jez to marry their daughter. People were beginning to think *we* were a couple...'

Bride

'No surprise I'm making a speech, since, as most of you will know, I like to have my say! Which is partly why my mother deserves extra special thanks for helping us organize today in spite of all the arguments. As usual she managed to calm me down and make today perfect. Thank you so much, mum.'

'I'd like to thank a whole host of people, including of course both Daniel and my parents – without whom we'd be sitting in the park eating fish and chips off our laps today! Also to my darling sister, whose legendary calming influence has been invaluable on so many occasions during the wedding-planning process! A special thank you also to Uncle Ron, whose generosity with his beautiful car meant that not only did I get to the church in style and on time, but also that I avoided the amused looks of strangers on the number 13 bus!'

'There is an unsung heroine of this wedding. I'd really like to say a few words of thanks to Carmen who made the beautiful dress I'm wearing. Carmen, without your skill and vision, I can't imagine that today would have been half as enjoyable. Throughout the whole dress-making saga you kept reassuring me that it would all be all right, and though I didn't believe you then, watching Ross's face light up as I walked down the aisle, I was so glad I listened to you. Thanks.'

Chief bridesmaid

'As chief bridesmaid I know it's my duty to get horribly drunk and stare in wonder and envy at the gorgeous bride we see here before us, while wondering when it'll be my turn. But before that happens, and I've still got a clear head, I'd like to say an enormous thank you to both sets of parents for making today happen and giving such a splendid party to mark the joining together of Lauren and Matthew. Additionally, Lauren's Aunty Carol also deserves a huge thank you for allowing this wonderful marquee to be pitched in her garden, and welcoming us all so generously. But most of all: Lauren you're my best friend and I want to thank you so much for the years of friendship as well as for choosing me to be your chief bridesmaid. It's been an incredible honour and I've loved every minute of it.'

About the families: Coming together

Father of bride

'It's a pleasure to be able to welcome you all here to celebrate the marriage of Jessica and Nick. One of the best things about today is that we've been able to bring all our family and friends together to mark this joyous occasion. We hope that you'll all thoroughly enjoy our special day.'

'Weddings are a marvellous excuse for a big party, and today is no exception. We have a simply enormous crowd here – aunts, uncles, cousins, friends... I think I even recognize a few of you!'

'They say that one of the best things about weddings is the way they bring families together. Well, that's certainly true of this one. People have come here today from far and wide – France, the US, Spain... I believe there may even be some from Manchester.'

'Seeing all the members of my family in one place is quite a novelty. Modern life is so busy that we're all usually rushing off in separate directions. The celebration of Polly and Nathan's marriage gives us the chance to relax and enjoy each other's company.'

Groom

'Weddings are an interesting experience, not least because they're one of the rare occasions on which one's family and friends get together. In fact, this is the only occasion in living memory when my friends have spent an evening with my family. So I'd like to use this opportunity to announce a list of subjects that are banned tonight – politics, religion, the euro, sex – and, of course Arsenal's chances in the European Cup. They are going to win and that's the end of it. Apart from that – enjoy yourselves.'

'Weddings throw people together in the nicest possible way. It's great to see Laura's friends and my friends, Laura's family and my family, all celebrating our happy day. I want to thank you all for coming to our wedding and helping to make it such an enjoyable occasion.'

'Having my friends as wedding guests has certainly put them in a new light. I couldn't imagine them all suited and booted before and they probably feel the same about me. You all look a little bit uncomfortable lads – but don't worry, you scrub up nicely.'

Best man

'Being Tim's best man has been a real privilege, not least because I've had the chance to meet his and Sarah's families. They are delightful people and have really pulled out all the stops to put on a fantastic spread for all of us. So, lads, make sure that you behave yourselves – remember you're not at the stag night now.'

'The occasion of Charlotte and Matthew's wedding is also the first time that the first XI rugby team has been reunited since our university days. And in the spirit of friends reunited, I'd like you all to raise a yard of ale to the bride and groom. We will not, however, be dropping our trousers or singing any inappropriate songs.'

'I'm glad to see young and old having a good time today. And I look forward to seeing you all shake your booty on the dance floor.'

Bride

'Wow – what a lot of people! But at least I know you're a friendly audience. I'd like to thank you all so much for coming here today to take part in the celebration of our marriage. Weddings are real family occasions, and it's lovely to see so many aunts, uncles and cousins here, many of whom I haven't seen for an awfully long time – although I do wish some of you would stop patting me on the head and remarking on how much I've grown.'

'I'd like to thank everyone who's complimented me on my dress and I have to say that, in the words of the song, you're all looking wonderful tonight. I never realized I had such well-dressed, good-looking family and friends. There's definitely some Kate Mosses and Brad Pitts out there.'

'Today, all the important people in my life are here. My family, my friends, and of course, Tom's family and friends. Being surrounded by the people we love the most is fantastic. Without your help and support, I don't think we could have got this far, and we hope you all enjoy yourselves today as much as we're going to.'

'All my friends are here tonight and I couldn't be happier to see them – although I'm not sure if they feel the same way about me, as I've been in a frenzy of pre-wedding anxiety for the last six months. Thanks girls, I really could not have done it without you. All that remains to say is just make sure you have a fantastic time.'

Chief bridesmaid
'Being at Sally and George's wedding is a real "friends reunited" experience. There are people here tonight who haven't been together since we did our A' levels. It takes me back to the days of big hair, cocktails and Wham! songs – well, I'll definitely be requesting "Club Tropicana" later and I hope you'll join me for a boogie.'

'Seeing Paul and Harriet's families together is an interesting experience. I can certainly see where they both get their brains and good looks from, not to mention their limitless capacity for partying.'

'As some of you may know, Ella and Anthony met when we were all working together, and it's great to see that so many people from our old office have turned up here today. We'll have to get together round the photocopier for a good gossip later on.'

About the families: Great mums

Father of the bride
'I stand here today, a proud father and a proud husband. I've already said how beautiful my daughter looks. But none of us would be here today without the great organizational skills, not to mention diplomatic abilities of my wonderful wife. The fact that she can arrange all of this and still look as young and beautiful as the day I married her is one of the reasons I love her so very much. Thank you, sweetheart.'

'Ladies and gentlemen, many of you have kindly commented to me on how beautiful Lisa looks today and I can only agree wholeheartedly. There is, of course, an explanation for this: she doesn't carry any of my genes, just those of my beautiful wife. So please be upstanding and drink a toast to the other belle of the ball, Lucy.'

Groom

'Ladies and gentlemen, the first time I set eyes on Katy's mum, I wondered why Katy hadn't told me she had a twin sister. It was quite obvious where Katy gets her looks (quite where her temper comes from, I don't know!). But I would like to say a big thank you to Katy's mum for supporting us through the traumas and tribulations of planning this wedding. Please be upstanding and drink a toast to Katy's mum…'

'As some of you know, my mum brought me up single-handedly after my dad died. I think she did a reasonable job (!) and I would just like to say: thanks mum. I know I wasn't the easiest child (though I still don't think they should have expelled me for that little misunderstanding involving the school cat and a firework). Mum has stuck by me through countless such traumas – in fact, she's probably delighted to get me off her hands! So these [flowers in hand] are for you.'

Best man

'Matt's mum has always been my kind of lady. None of my girlfriends made me cakes when I went round to their houses. It is said that the way to a man's heart is through his stomach and she certainly knew how to pull my heart strings.'

'After my mum died, I used to spend most of my time round at John's house after school. There was always a place at the table laid out for me and a warm welcome from his mum. I can still smell her chocolate cake even now. Thanks Mrs Smith, or should I say mum?'

Chief bridesmaid

'Gill's mum has always been a special mum, and not just to Gill. Whenever us kids were in trouble, it was always Gill's mum we turned to. She's always been there to sort out no end of problems, from cut knees to broken hearts. She's no different today. Even at the hen night, she was busy making sure we all got home safely in taxis from the nightclub, and let me tell you, there aren't many mums who can boogie the night away like she can!'

'As chief bridesmaid, I would just like to say a special thank you to Justine's mum. Justine and Jamie will tell you they organized the whole thing, but we all know what hopeless liars they are! Justine's mum has been the inspiration and the guiding light for much of what has happened today, not to mention chief-shoulder-to-cry-on when the bridesmaids' dresses didn't fit and my little nephew Jake decided to add some colour to the veil with his new felt-tips!'

About the families: To the mums and dads

Groom

'I owe a big thank you to my own mum and dad for helping me in so many ways to make this day so special, and in return I can assure you only the finest nursing home awaits you! And to my new set of parents, what can I say? You have raised Clare to be the most kind-hearted, loving and considerate woman a man could ever hope to meet, and for this I'm truly grateful. I'd also like to show my appreciation for allowing me to marry your daughter, and to express my special thanks for that steamy night in the back of Geoff's Ford Cortina 27 years ago, that brought your daughter into this world and made this whole wedding possible!'

Bride

'And so, mum, dad, the time has finally come for me to fly the nest. Obviously I can see you're heartbroken – even though the minute after Aaron and I told you about our engagement, you were already making plans to convert "my" bedroom into a sauna. And because I know that deep down you are so anxious for me not to leave, you'll be pleased to hear that we have decided to postpone moving for a few months until we find that perfect home… Only kidding! But looking at the shade of white you've just turned, I think we've found the perfect wall colour for our new flat!'

About the families: Now we're one big family

Father of the bride

'Coming from a small family myself, the prospect of acquiring such a large new extended family is a little daunting – especially with all those new names and birthdays to remember. When I got married myself, I thought the wife and in-laws were a major addition to the Jones family – but I now seem to have acquired half the population of a small, rapidly expanding country!
But whether there are five or fifteen of you, I can truthfully say that we're thrilled for Lucy to be marrying into such a generous and warm bunch of people, and we're sure that she's got enough love to give to you all.'

'Since Jenny and Glen announced they were getting hitched, Glen's family have been nothing but welcoming and open. They have been willing to share everything with us, including the cost of the celebrations. To me, today represents not only the union of our children, but also the coming together of our two wonderful families.'

Bride

'I must say that at first I was slightly overwhelmed at the thought of acquiring such a large new family, but after having spent some time with you all I have come to the conclusion that all that stuff about mad aunts and spoilt cousins Jake spent so long telling me about must be in his head…
Only kidding! I could not have asked for a better lot to marry into, which is just as well, as we've decided that by combining our two families, we're going to stage our own mini-Olympics this summer…'

Groom

'Michelle is very close to each of her four sisters, and I know for sure – through witnessing numerous sobbing sessions – that it's going to be very hard on her to move away from you and move in with me. Therefore I want you all to know that our house is open to each and every one of you whenever you like. However, I hope that, as my loving sisters-in-law, you won't insist on me joining in with all your nights of toenail painting and bikini-line waxing!'

Declarations of love

Drop these romantic or poetic extracts into your speech for an extra-special effect.

Romantic

The following letter was written by French intellectual Simone de Beauvoir to her partner and fellow philosopher, Jean-Paul Sartre. Their relationship lasted an inspiring 51 years.

'I'm altogether immersed in the happiness I derive from seeing you. Nothing else counts. I have you – little all-precious one, little beloved one – as much today as the day before yesterday when I could see you, and I'll have you till the day I die. After that, nothing of all that may happen to me really has any importance. Not only am I not sad, I'm even deeply happy and secure. Even the tenderest memories – of all your dear expressions, or your little arms cradling the pillow in the morning – aren't painful to me. I feel myself all enfolded and sustained by your love.'

For all true romantics, here's the perfect expression of love. This letter was written by the writer Katherine Mansfield to her husband, the writer and critic John Middleton Murray:

Dear John
My love for you tonight is so deep and tender that it seems to be outside myself as well. I am fast shut up like a little lake in the embrace of some big mountains. If you were to climb up the mountains, you would see me down below, deep and shining — and quite fathomless, my dear. You might drop your heart into me and you'd never hear it touch bottom.
I love you — I love you — Goodnight.

Poetic

Preface this poem with the following dedication: 'I'd like to dedicate the following poem, written by Anne Bradstreet, to my dear and loving husband...'

If ever two were one, then surely we.
If ever man were loved by wife, then thee;
If ever wife was happy in a man.
Compare with me ye women if you can.
I prize thy love more than whole mines of gold.
Or all the riches that the East doth hold.
My love is such that rivers cannot quench.
Nor ought but love from thee, give recompense.
Thy love is such I can no way repay,
The heavens reward thee manifold I pray.

Then while we live, in love let's so persevere,
That when we live no more, we may live ever.

'When we came across this poem, 'I Want You' by Arthur
L Gillom, it summed up beautifully what we mean to each
other. For that reason, we've chosen an extract and decided
to read alternate verses...'

I want you when the day is at its noontime.
Sun-steeped and quiet, or drenched with sheets of rain:
I want you when the roses bloom in June-time:
I want you when the violets come again.

I want you when my soul is thrilled with passion;
I want you when I'm weary and depressed;
I want you when in lazy, slumberous fashion
My senses need the haven of your breast.

I want you when through field and wood I'm roaming;
I want you when I'm standing on the shore;
I want you when the summer birds are homing –
And when they've flown I want you more and more.

I want you, dear, through every changing season;
I want you with a tear or with a smile;
I want you more than any rhyme or reason –
I want you, want you, want you – all the while.

Traditional, old-fashioned

'I was never on the look-out for someone like my wife because I had no idea such a wonderful combination of qualities could exist in one person. Carole, you are everything I never knew I wanted.'

'I consider myself the luckiest man/woman alive… because I had the good fortune to fall in love with my greatest friend.'

'Marriage is an exciting and daunting prospect for anyone. But as we set off down the long and winding road together, I know that with Catherine by my side, I could not wish for a wiser, kinder guide and companion.'

'I've always known Marcelle was the girl for me. After all, what's there not to like? But what I've never quite understood is what's in it for her. Meeting and being with her has been like a fantastic dream come true. I just hope I never wake up…'

'I want to thank Paul for all the joy and warmth and strength we have already shared, and for all the plans we have made and the pleasures that lie ahead. But most of all I want to thank him for saying "Yes".'

'In preparation for this moment, I've been researching hard to come up with one great poetic phrase that would eloquently sum up everything that I feel about you, and how much this moment means to me. But nothing quite expressed what I wanted to say, so let me keep it old-fashioned and say, before all our family and friends today: "I love you".'

Declarations of love: Famous words

'In the words of David Beckham: "She rocks my world"!'

'As Elizabeth Barrett Browning once wrote: "How do I love thee? Let me count the ways. I love thee to the depth and breadth and height my soul can reach".'

'Edward VIII made one of the famous declarations of love ever when he announced to the nation: "I have found it impossible to carry the heavy burden of responsibility and to discharge my duties as King as I would wish to do without the help and support of the woman I love." I know that I too, if push came to shove, would gladly lay down my country for my wife (or in fact lay down in the country *with* my wife).'

When I think of my wife, I'm reminded of the passionate letters exchanged by the poet Dylan Thomas and his wife Caitlin. Of course I substitute her name for Caitlin's when I read lines like these: "Caitlin. Just to write down your name like that. Caitlin. I don't have to say My dear, My darling, My sweetheart, though I do say these words, to you in myself, all day and night. Caitlin. And all the words are in that one word".'

Declarations of love: With a difference

'The mysterious beauty of my new wife recalls for me these wonderfully poetic lines by the poet e. e. cummings: "Only something in me understands/The voice of your eyes is deeper than all roses/Nobody, not even the rain, has such small hands".'

'Paul, since I have started loving you, I've seen the whole world in a new light. As the poet Krishnamurti wrote: "Love is the answer, it changes everything. The moment you have in your heart this extraordinary thing called love and feel the depth, the delight, the ecstasy of it, you will discover that for you the world is transformed".'

'When I read these words by Erica Jong, they really rang true for me. "Do you want me to tell you something really subversive? Love is everything it's cracked up to be. That's why people are so cynical about it. It really is worth fighting for, being brave for, risking everything for. And the trouble is, if you don't risk everything, you risk even more".'

'In the words of the French poet Jadice Holsen: *"Je ne garde que le t de je t'aime"*. Which might be translated as "I wish to keep only the you of I love you".'

People we miss: They couldn't be here...

Father of bride

'It's wonderful to see so many people who've travelled so far to come and join us in our celebrations today. Sadly, Bob and Alice were unable to get over from Australia, and they are sorely missed today. But I know that they're thinking about us today, and raising a glass to Kate and Jim even as we speak. Or they will when they wake up, anyway!'

'I speak for everyone when I say how much we miss my mum, who sadly can't be with us today because of ill-health. Mary has always been the life and soul of the party, so she'll be particularly upset to miss out on today's knees-up! But thanks to the wonders of technology, we'll be going round to visit her tomorrow with edited video highlights of today's action...'

Groom

'In case you're wondering... Andy, my first choice for best man, can't be here to perform his duties because of a broken leg. Andy insists his accident occurred whilst bull-running in Pamplona, but my sources inform me that he actually dropped an iron on his foot, aggravating an old step aerobics injury... While we all wish him well, it's a relief to introduce my next oldest friend, Pete, who has slightly less dirt on me...'

'Just a quick word about my brother Jim, who can't be with us today. He told us he was training with the British Olympic team in Colorado, but I had doubts when a present arrived this morning: two Woodbines and a shirt made out of mail-bags.'

Best man

'Let me tell you, the run-up to this wedding was really hectic, with all sorts of unexpected last-minute changes. Most drastic of all was when Liz decided to swap her actual choice of groom. So out went "Si", her slovenly, hopelessly-turned-out, never-on-time grunt of a partner these last seven years. And in came "Simon", this strange new man you see before you: impeccably dressed, polite, attentive… and EARLY!'

'Although I have known Russell for ten years, there is someone else who's known him even longer. Nick went to primary school with Russell and has been causing mischief with him ever since, but unfortunately could not be here today. Contrary to popular belief, Russell has not amputated Nick's legs in a desperate attempt to avoid the spectacle of him attempting to body-pop later on – Nick is currently acting as best man at his brother's wedding. Hard luck, Russell, looks like you're stuck with me instead. Naked Twister, anyone?'

Bride

'You may have noticed that my dear friend Theresa is not here today to perform her usual role of hand-holder and general calming influence over proceedings. I can assure you, however, that she has a more than adequate excuse for missing the celebrations as she gave birth to a lovely baby boy, Josh, just four days ago. Look's like it'll be a hard day's night for all of us!'

People we miss: Recent bereavement

Father of bride

'A wedding is a time for joy and fun, with friends and family gathered to see the happy couple off as they embark on a new, shared life. But it is a time, too, when our thoughts inevitably turn to those people who cannot be with us today, and especially those who have left this life. And it is an especially poignant time for those whose own partners have passed on too. So let's just take a moment to remember [gives name of bereaved]. We remember them with love and pride, and we ask for their blessing.'

'The speech I'm making now should really be made by my brother Hal, Janine's father, but sadly he cannot be with us. Janine is his only daughter, and she meant the absolute world to him. He would have loved today's big occasion, I'm sure you'll agree. I can picture him swanning around in the loudest tie he could lay his hands on, sneaking out for a swift drink before the service, and holding the floor with those risqué jokes that somehow only he seemed to be able to get away with. I know too that he would have gone around all day with the biggest, stupidest, proudest grin on his face. I am honoured to have been asked to fill Bob's place, even as I am saddened by the circumstances. We all miss him. But I know that he would want you all to enjoy the day and give all your best wishes to the happy couple.'

Groom

'As many of you will know, our family has recently suffered a terrible blow with the unexpected and tragic death of my father Brian. For some time we even wondered whether it would be appropriate to postpone the wedding, as a mark of respect. But when we talked it over, everyone was in agreement that the occasion would provide a great opportunity to share our thoughts and feelings about Brian – and that wherever we were all gathered, Brian would be there in spirit with us too. So perhaps you will understand if I am sad that he cannot be here to share this day with me – though in marrying Caitlin, I am the luckiest man alive. But I and all my family draw great comfort from the fact that we are surrounded by people who knew him and loved him and remember him, and I know that this day – which he was so looking forward to – will be all the richer as a result.'

'Now if my mum could be here today, I know what she'd say: "Nice spread, son, but for goodness' sake stand up straight and get your hair cut"!'

Best man

'I am honoured to be standing here as best man for Tom,
though I am mindful that this place belonged by rights to
Gary, who tragically cannot be with us. Perhaps in choosing
me Tom thought he would be getting off lightly, because of
course, I didn't go to school or spend my childhood with
Tom, as Gary did. On the other hand, the telephone is a
wonderful thing, and many people have been kind enough
to come forward with their reminiscences. So I don't think
we'll be too short on suitable material – and before I go
any further, I'd like to say a special thank you for her candour
(and her Polaroids) to Sally.'

Bride

'It is a great sadness that my parents cannot be here today
to see Graham and me finally making it down the aisle.
They both knew and loved Graham, and though neither mum
nor dad ever put any pressure on us, I know it was their
fondest wish that the two of us should get married in
church, as we have done here today. So I'd like to dedicate
this day to their memory, and to say an enormous thank you
to them both for all the love and patience they showed to
me and my brothers and sisters while we were growing up.
And if I ever have children, and if I can do half as good a job
as a parent, then I'll have done very well...'

'My mum and I were always very close, and I know that we
would have spent the months leading up to this wedding
busily making plans and drawing up lists and traipsing round

all the dress shops comparing fabrics. So when she died last year, I thought it would be a great sadness to go through all these preparations without her. Of course, I missed her wisdom and her wit at every turn, but I had a strong sense that her presence was guiding me the whole time. So thanks for your help, mum. Anything that goes well today is down to you – I'll take credit for the mistakes!'

'At this point I'd like to take a moment to mention my best friend Katie, who cannot be here today because of a bereavement in her own family. Our thoughts are with her at this difficult time, and we send her and her family all our love and condolences.'

Chief bridesmaid

'A wedding is not only a happy celebration but also a time to remember the people who are important in your life. And so let us all pause for a moment and say a silent prayer for all those here today who are missing loved ones, especially [give names if appropriate].'

'I was going to share the job of chief bridesmaid with Claire's childhood friend Alice. Alice had been seriously ill for some time, however, and sadly she passed away last month. Everyone who knew her, will always remember the incredible zest for life she had and her boundless energy. And I know that right now, she's looking down and saying: "Just get on with it girl, and make sure you grab the last bottle of champagne"!'

People we miss: Greetings from...

Father of the bride

'I have here a message from my brother Ted, who cannot be here today because of poor health. Ted has asked me to pass on his best wishes to the happy couple, and to remind Gavin that everyone here would surely be delighted to hear his charming Marmite and Swarfega story... Are you alright, Gavin? You look a trifle pale...'

'I'd like to read now a postcard from my son, Colin – Toby's brother – who's currently on active service at an undisclosed location (or so he says). "Sorry I can't be there bruv, but these Hollywood award ceremonies are a real killer. I swear if I have to attend another star-studded, all-night pool party, I'm going to go mad! Anyway, enjoy tonight's barn dance"...'

Groom

'I have here a note from my stepmum, Carole, who wanted to be here today but decided that there is enough tension in the world today without causing another ruck! Seriously though, folks, she sends her love and best wishes to me and Paula, and we're grateful for her kind thoughts and her lovely flowers.'

'My wife and I want to say a big thank you to Father Michael, who stepped in at the last minute in place of our friend Father Andrew, who was called away on a parish emergency at the eleventh hour. Father Michael tells me Andrew has just been in touch to say: "Sorry I couldn't get to the church on time – but just you try and stop me doing the christening"!'

Best man

'And now I'd like to read a couple of telegrams. The first one says: "Sorry I couldn't be there Bob, but you know how funny Michael gets about these things. Still, we'll always have that night of 'fatal attraction' in Merthyr Tydfil…" And that's signed… "Catherine Z-J"…'

'And here's a message from our old schoolmate, Pete Best: "Sorry I couldn't make it to your big day, Baz, but there's loads of really good telly on this afternoon. In fact, I can't believe you chose a wedding date that overlapped with the "Hollyoaks" omnibus! Still, hopefully I'll have worked out how to programme the video in time for your next wedding"… Ahem, thanks very much Pete – that's absolutely charming…'

Bride

'I have here a letter from my dad who wasn't able to be here today. "Dearest Sarah, I'm so sorry not to be there for your special day but – as we both agreed – it's probably for the best. But I want you to know how much I love you and am thinking of you both on this wonderful occasion. It's hard for a father to lose his only daughter – but Jake is a decent, kind man and I am happy to see you in such safe hands. I wish you both every happiness for your life together".'

'Finally, I'd like to just read a quick note from my best friend Patsy, who decided not to attend my wedding for the very feeble reason that she's currently in labour. It says: "Good luck, Meg. OW! OW! OOOOOOW!" Not much of a message really, but I suppose it's the thought that counts…'

The stag night: Consequences

Groom

'I want to take a moment to talk about the stag weekend Mike organized for me and the lads in Blackpool. The weekend was the usual mix of culture and sophistication. But it also reminded me of how lucky I am, marrying Anna. As I lay in the jacuzzi, smoking a cigar and drinking champagne, I turned to Roxanne and said, "Do you know? My wife-to-be is the most understanding woman I've ever met." 'Er… judging by her face, though, I think I might have been a bit hasty there.'

Best man

'It's great to see so many of the lads who went on the stag weekend here today. It's a shame that the rest of them couldn't get bail, though. We'll drink a toast to the Skegness Six later. And their lawyer tells me that they've got a strong case. As long as the horse makes a full recovery, then the farmer will drop most of the charges. But seriously, it was a great weekend and it gave Rob a chance to let off some steam before marrying Lisa. Raquel says "Hi" by the way, Rob.'

The stag night: Worries beforehand

Groom

'I must admit, I was a little bit nervous about what the lads, especially Dave my best man, might have in store for me for the stag night. I'd heard stories about guys being tied naked to lamp posts or being forced to eat whipped cream off the bare chest of a young, nubile stripper. Thankfully none of that happened on our weekend away in Bognor.

'In fact, it was two days of non-stop laughs. A chance to spend quality time with some of my mates whom I haven't seen enough of recently. I'll never forget you all, especially as you insisted I had all of your names tattooed on to my posterior. Don't worry, sweetheart, I can have them lasered off...'

Best man

'I must say that I was a little surprised – and almost disappointed – that Rob was so nervous and worried about the stag weekend. In fact, he was still nervous and worried as we got on the train to Margate on Friday night. Mysteriously, though, after only a couple of hours his nerves seemed to have disappeared, as had a dozen cans of strong continental lager. And by the time we reached Saucy Sue's, it was Rob who was telling *me* to stop worrying. Don't worry about the money, he said. Don't worry about explaining this to Anna, he said. In fact, stop worrying was all he could say!'

The stag night: What we really got up to

Groom

'I expect you're all wondering what we got up to on the stag weekend. I'm sure that you're all desperate to know some of the more salacious details. You'd love to know about some of the depraved and debauched behaviour that went on. Well, there's an old saying that goes, "What goes on tour, stays on tour." This is a solemn and unspoken agreement, entered into by anyone attending such an event.

'Although, I must say, anyone who has ever used this as an excuse also knows the real reason behind it. It is, in fact, a great way of covering up the fact that you can't remember a single detail about the weekend, other than the first hour of the journey. The rest is just an expensive blur...'

Best man

'And so on to the most important part of my speech. A blow-by-blow account of exactly what went on at the stag do. I expect you're all dying to know the gory details. I'd really like to tell you how Rob found himself pole-dancing with two girls from the Swedish netball team; how he had to be dragged out of the tattoo parlour; how he was arrested for "acts of a lewd and lascivious nature" on the sea front; and of how he chatted up a rhododendron bush for three hours outside the nightclub. [pause] I'd really like to tell you all about that… but I can't. As usual Rob had two Bacardi Breezers and passed out at nine o'clock.'

'What did we get up to on the stag night, I hear you ask? Did Bill disgrace himself? Did the lads stitch him up? I'm saying nothing. My lips are sealed. All I'm going to say, Bill, is I'm glad to see your eyebrows have grown back!'

The stag night: Saying sorry

Groom

'I'd like to take this opportunity to say sorry for what went on at the stag weekend. First of all, sorry to the people of Skegness. I really hope that the pier was insured. Secondly to the local constabulary. I'm sure that with some disinfectant and elbow-grease the stains will come out of the seats. Thirdly to my best man, Tim, who went to all the trouble of organizing the weekend, only to be chained to a set of railings 20 minutes into the celebrations and left to fend for himself. How is the frost-bite, Tim? 'But lastly, sorry to my wife, Anna. Thanks to you, I won't have to do a stag night ever again.'

Best man

'They always say that it's better to regret the things you have done, than regret the things that you haven't. With that in mind, everyone who went on the stag do should be feeling a terrible sense of regret. Because we did it all. Drink, drugs (well Nurofen), loose women, lewd behaviour, and a small amount of criminal damage. (And we all thought our student sign-stealing days were behind us, eh, lads?)
'But there's one person who shouldn't feel regret and has nothing to apologize for. That is, of course, the groom Paul. Despite our best efforts his conscience is clean. He really must love Jane very, very much!'

The stag night: Telegrams

Groom

'I've just got a couple of telegrams to read out. I know this is usually the best man's job, but these are actually addressed to him. The first reads: "Dear Mr Thomas. Further to your enquiries about tattoo removal, I enclose a price list. Please note that due to the sensitive nature of…" Er, that must be from the stag do, I guess. You can read that later, Tim. The second reads: "Dear Mr Thomas, in the light of your exemplary character witnesses, we are willing to waive the charges, on the condition that you return the regimental goat within two working days. Yours, Lieutenant-Colonel F. P. Farthington-Smythe."

'Any comment on those, Tim?'

Best man

'I've just got a couple of telegrams to read out. One is all the way from Marseille in France, where I think, you went on holiday a couple of years ago Dan, didn't you? Anyway, it reads: "Allo Daniel. Ow are you? I mees zat you no write to mee no more. Les enfants, zey cry all zee time and zey miss zere Papa. Ven you are returning a France? I vant to faire l'amour with you! Encore! Encore"!'

'Here's another cheery message from some old friends: "Best of luck on the big day, Slasher. The slammer's a lonelier place without yer. Hope it all goes well with the new lovely lady and cheers for the snout. Can't wait to visit when we all get out." And that's signed: "The boys on C Wing".'

About the relationship:
They've known each other since...

Father of the bride/Best man/Chief bridesmaid

'These two have known each other since they were children. Even then there was quite a spark between them – although that's probably because Angela liked to use Rick as a human guinea pig in her chemistry experiments…'

'They've known each other since Clara went up to Ben in the student union bar and asked him to hold her pint while she went to the loo. He fell in love on the spot there and then.'

'They've known each other since they bumped into one another at the launderette while at college. A perfectly normal way to meet someone, I suppose. Made remarkable only because that was the only day, in the three years that he was there, that Rob went anywhere near a launderette.'

'The happy couple have known each other ever since they bumped into one another in the high street of Anna's home town. A romantic way to meet, I guess, except Anna was in her car and Rob was on his bike at the time!'

About the relationship:
I wouldn't say they're romantic, but...

Father of the bride/Best man/Chief bridesmaid

'Dan is determined that the honeymoon, which he has organized, will be truly romantic. He's planning walks on deserted beaches; downing cocktails and sampling the local cuisine. It's a secret, so I won't give too much away. Except to say that the cycle shop's done really well this month...'

'Jane once said that it's the wee things Ralph does that makes him so special. That's funny because at infants' school it was the wee Ralph did that made him special.'

'I wouldn't say the groom is romantic but I did hear he presented his lovely bride with three dozen roses in bed on Valentine's Day. Unfortunately the chocolate melted on to the sheets, which killed the mood a little...'

'We all know Phil likes to take risks and he's already told me how, on the flight to their honeymoon, he's planning to do something naughty in the loo. Honestly, Phil, smoking's very bad for you!'

'I wouldn't say the bride and groom were particularly romantic. Instead of a flash engagement ring, they decided to buy something for the flat. In fact it's only because her parents came to the rescue that you're not currently being addressed by the dishwasher!'

About the relationship: Great team

Father of the bride

'There is great teamwork in everything that they do. Whether it's redecorating the bathroom or choosing a honeymoon, they are able to work together at close quarters for hours on end without a sign of irritation or tension...'

'Helen and I knew right from the outset that these two would make a great team, and we've been proved right. They work hard for each other and don't seem to grumble or moan about anything. And that is the sign of a winning team. This is, of course, a whole new concept to Gerry, him being a Tottenham fan and all...'

'Bobby and Belinda make a perfect team. They always put each other first, and never let other worries get in the way of their relationship. When one of them has a success, the other is there to celebrate. And when one of them is down, the other is there to comfort them. I'm constantly amazed by their closeness and real, heartfelt intimacy.'

Groom

'What I really love about my relationship with Laura is that we make a really great team. We trust and support one another, and we each know that, come what may, the other will be there for them. I know that marriage is not all fun and laughter like today, but I know too that my wife and I have the strength to deal with any difficulties that life may throw at us.'

Best man

'I'm sure that Rob and Anna are going to make a great team. Rob has always been good at team sports. I remember at school when they were asking for volunteers for the hockey team, he volunteered immediately and went on to be the hero of the side. He did admit to me recently, though, that the reason he volunteered was that he thought hockey was a mixed sport at our school.'

'Derek and Ellie will make a great team, I'm sure. Derek's been involved in team sports since school. He was linesman for the footie team, scorer for the cricket team and sponge man and physio for the chess team…'

Bride

'I've never really been a fan of team sports myself, but since I've met Chris I can see the benefits. We rely on each other totally and have the same goals and help each other achieve them. We don't squabble when the chips are down and there are no recriminations if things don't go the way we planned.'

Chief bridesmaid

'If you approach marriage with the same team spirit you've shown in all of the things we've done together, Pam, and you won't go far wrong. Ever since I've known you you've been a great team player, whether it was in the girl guides, netball or the drinking team at college. Your selflessness and determination, I'm sure, are what attracted Jonathan to you… That and the fact that you can drink most rugby players under the table…'

About the relationship:
How they've changed each other...

Father of the bride/Best man/Chief bridesmaid

'What you are looking at here today is a couple that make a great pair. Like cheese and onion. Or salt and vinegar. And like a bag of crisps left open, since Ben met Angie, he's gone all soft.'

'Since Keith and Lynne have been together you can see the effect they've had on each other. Keith no longer wears the same T-shirt every day; his "Star Trek" collection is in storage and his feet smell less. And as for Lynne, she has... lowered her expectations!'

'We used to worry about Ian living on his own because we knew the only thing he could cook was beans on toast. Then Sonja came along and he told us how she had revolutionized his diet. So we went round for lunch: beans on *granary* toast!'

Groom/Bride

'The greatest influence Carrie has had on me is on my spending. I don't waste my salary in the pub any more – I waste hers too!'

'Since meeting Bill, I can say that I've truly learnt to love the beautiful game. It's called "Hide the remote control five minutes before Match of the Day".'

About the relationship:
No stopping them now...

'I think you'll all agree that the two of them together will make an awesome team. With his drive, determination and passion for DIY, and her ability to look interested, there'll be no stopping them...'

'Just before we set off for the church this morning, Miles turned to me and said, "Me and Helen, there's no stopping us now." "There is," I said. "We've got ten minutes to get to the church and your car's got a flat..."'

'I look at the two of you and think to myself, what a wonderful life you have in front of you. There's no stopping you now. The only thing I would advise, Jeff – it's an old cliché, but it's true – is never go to bed on an argument. You never know if you're going to wake up otherwise...'

'Looking at these two, I think that you'll agree that there's no stopping a couple like them. Individually they were successful, but together they can achieve anything, go anywhere and be anybody they want to be. I look forward to watching the two of you enjoying your life together, and I feel privileged to be a part of it by being here today...'

'There's no stopping them now. Unless, of course, Rob's court hearing goes the wrong way...'

About the relationship: Not a bed of roses

Best man

'Marriage is not always a bed of roses. I learnt this myself when, after a fearsome argument with my beloved, I was forced to sleep in the flowerbed for the night.'

'As you embark on your journey together as man and wife, I know everyone here joins me in wishing you health and happiness over the coming years. That said, it's important to recognize that there are likely to be lows as well as highs. As anyone who's ever got hitched will tell you, marriage is no bed of roses. And bearing in mind Brendan's excruciating sax playing, these may come sooner than you think…'

Father of the bride

'In many ways all marriages are like a bed of roses. But not in the traditional way that most people think of when they hear that phrase. I'm talking more from a horticultural point of view. Just as roses do, a marriage needs constant attention, careful maintenance and wholesome sustenance. Each rose needs to be monitored and checked, so that any sign of blight can be quickly nipped in the bud. Each flower needs gentle encouragement. And, if all of those things happen, each turns into a wonderful, awe-inspiring thing that radiates beauty and brings pleasure and satisfaction to those who are lucky enough to witness it…'

'My marriage to Helen's mother wasn't always a bed of roses. It was something that, at times, we had to really work at. Over the last 20 years we've shared some wonderful times: our first married Christmas, moving into our first home, Anna being born, Sunderland winning the FA Cup in 1973. But we've had our rocky times as well. Helen's illness, the car crash, the burglary and, of course, Sunderland getting relegated in 1983. But, I guess what I'm trying to say is, even though it hasn't been a bed of roses all the way through, it has been a truly wonderful experience. And I hope and pray that your marriage is the same, because I wouldn't change a single minute of mine...'

'Your marriage may not always be a bed of roses, but in my experience that's a great thing. Because if you don't have low points, you're never going to fall out with each other. And if you don't fall out, you can't spend a whole Saturday afternoon making up. And where would a marriage be without that!'

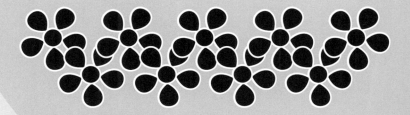

Advice for the honeymoon:
On my honeymoon...

Father of the bride
'Before I left for my own honeymoon, my father gave me two pieces of advice. Number one, don't forget to take protection with you, and number two, make sure your underwear befits the occasion. How right he was: both the umbrella and the thermal vest came in very handy during our week in Bognor.'

Groom
'When I was trying to decide where to take Karen for our honeymoon, I asked my father-in-law for some advice. He said to me: "Why not take her somewhere hot and steamy she's never been before?" So I am pleased to announce that we are honeymooning in the kitchen.'

Best man
'I remember Dave taking me aside just before I left for my honeymoon and advising me to eat lots of bananas for their high energy content. You should have no trouble getting tropical fruit where you're going, but just in case [hands paper to groom] here's the phone number for the local Viagra dealer.'

Advice for the honeymoon: Before you go

Father of the bride

'Before you whisk my daughter off to the sun, I'd like to offer you some advice. Don't let her drink too much and do karaoke; remember to tell her she looks brown, even if she's gone a lovely shade of embarrassed lobster; and above all, never, ever laugh at her passport photo!'

Groom

'I didn't think things could get any better than this. Not only have I met and married the woman of my dreams, but also you've all helped to make today perfect for both of us. And just now I received the best news of all… we've got access to Premiership football in our hotel room!'

Best man

'We've eaten, drunk, danced and sung (and that was just on the stag night!) and it's almost time for you two to get on the plane and head off together on your honeymoon.
And although you've got tons of fantastic presents to open, I bet I can guess exactly what Dave's most looking forward to unwrapping!'

Advice for the honeymoon:
Keep expectations in check

Father of the bride

'Dave, you're probably expecting a fortnight of relaxation and carefree abandon, but take it from me as one who knows, if your back recovers after hauling Karen's suitcases around the airport, you'll soon put it out again when she asks you to load up the shop's worth of souvenirs she'll want to take home.'

Best man

'Having been on holiday with Don myself, Petra, I think it's important that you double-check you've got everything packed to make it the holiday of a lifetime. I'm talking, of course, about those special accessories that'll help the nights go as smoothly as the days… earplugs. Now wish them well, Petra and her amazing chainsaw-snoring husband, Don!'

Chief bridesmaid

'As Janine's closest friend, Alex, I feel it my duty to give you some words of advice for your honeymoon. First, she will *not* find your "Kiss Me Quick" hat amusing; second – whatever she says – she *cannot* walk in her platform flip-flops; and third, I can say with conviction that Janine, Baileys and champagne do *not* mix.'

Advice for the honeymoon:
Send us a postcard

Father of the bride

'As you get ready for your first holiday as man and wife, I want to wish you a very happy honeymoon. Don't think of us at home, fretting over how we're going to pay for today. And don't forget to send us a postcard. It'll contrast nicely with all the bills on the doormat!'

'Of course you'll be far too busy visiting historical ruins and scuba diving to call home every day, but perhaps you could send your old man a postcard just to let him know you're having a good time.'

Best man

'As Mike's best friend, I thought he'd appreciate my offer of accompanying him and Debs on honeymoon. Strangely, though, they both seemed a little reluctant to tell me where they're going. So I thought I'd do some undercover investigating, only to find that not only has the travel agent's number been cut out of the Yellow Pages, but it's also missing from Mike's address book and the Thompson Local...'

Making a marriage last: Marriage is like...

Father of the bride

'Marriage is like an Ordnance Survey map: although it's sometimes difficult to navigate, you'd be lost without it.'

'Marriage to me is like a log fire. When you feel cold, it heats you up, puts warmth in your heart and a glow on your cheeks.'

'On my silver wedding anniversary it occurred to me – a happily married homeowner – that marriage is much like a mortgage. It's expensive and stressful, and initially you may have to deny yourself life's luxuries to make it work. But after 25 years, it all pays off and you've got something you can truly call your own.'

'Marriage is like a pair of your granddad's old slippers, comfortable and familiar.'

'Marriage is like a sketchbook whose pages get filled up over the years. On your wedding day you begin with a blank sheet of paper and pencil, poised to create true beauty.'

Making a marriage last: Marriage is like...

Groom

'A wise man once told me that marriage can be compared to an umbrella. When the weather's fair, it's easy to forget you need it. But when it pours with rain, you'll be glad of the shelter from the storm.'

'My uncle Derek used to say to me that marriage is much like digging a hole. The more you put in, the more you'll get out. I checked with Aunty Jean though, and apparently he's never even been near the garden centre, let alone picked up a spade.'

Best man

'Marriage for men is much like a game of football. With skill and stamina you can last the distance. But dirty tackle will almost always get you sent off for an early bath!'

'My marriage often seems like an action movie. The plot is an emotional rollercoaster but, as the hapless hero, I always end up in the arms of the beautiful woman.'

'A good marriage is like a riding a unicycle. It's difficult to get the balance right, but it gets easier with practice and you'll be the envy of all your friends...'

'Marriage is like buying a new pair of trousers. A snug fit is usually best, but a bit of give often helps.'

Making a marriage last: Marriage is like...

Bride

'When Ian and I got engaged, I couldn't help but pay attention to all the horror stories about failed marriages and the scarily high divorce statistics. Feeling decidedly shaky, I asked my mum for some advice. She said to me that marriage is like a work of art. With dedication, passion, patience and conviction you can create something truly priceless. Today is just the beginning of our life together, and I'm honoured to have you all here on the first day that Ian and I start work on our masterpiece.'

Chief bridesmaid

'A good marriage is like a good novel. It has you hooked from day one, is awe-inspiring, impossible to put down and you never want it to end.'

'A loving marriage is much like a fingerprint. It identifies who you are and stays with you for ever.'

'Marriage is like a cocktail: at its best it can leave you feeling like dancing in the street and singing from the rooftops. Sometimes it comes with fireworks, and sometimes with a paper umbrella. Hmmm.'

Making a marriage last: My secret is...

Father of the bride

'Anna, your mother and I are so pleased that you and Roger have finally tied the knot, and although you've never taken any advice from me in the past, I'm hoping that today you'll make an exception. I've been married for 30 years, so believe me, I know what I'm talking about. The secret is simple: honesty, trust, love and affection.'

Best man

'Given that my own wife and I have been married for five years, I am in the rare position of being able to offer James advice on something that, for once, he does not know more about than me – the secret to making a marriage last. Always tell your wife you love her after making love. And wherever I am in the world, I always make sure I call Lizzie and tell her how much she means to me.'

Chief bridesmaid

'When Jan and I were growing up, we often used to wonder which of the two of us would get married first. Who would have believed that it would turn out to be me? And so, as chief bridesmaid, I thought I'd share my secret with you for a successful marriage. The trick is to treat your man like you'd treat a mushroom. Keep him in the dark for as long as possible and he'll flourish.'

Making a marriage last:
When the chips are down...

Father of the bride

'There are a few things I think you should know about Michelle. There will be times when she'll flip her lid and shout at you for no reason, hitting you over the head with her slippers. There will be times when she'll refuse to get out of bed for hours on end. On occasions like these there is only one cure. It comes wrapped in shiny paper, and it's called chocolate.'

Best man

'As you embark on the road to wedded bliss, here's some advice to you both on how to avoid the potholes. Walter, never say, "You're right, your bum does look big in that." Jenny, try not to laugh as Walter's scalp becomes more and more visible. Pre-empt heated driving arguments by keeping an A to Z in the car; and Jenny, understand that if Walter staggers to bed at 3am singing "I'm too sexy", it's bound to be my fault...'

Chief bridesmaid

'Today is about celebrating the love between Erica and Gary. Apart from the mystery of how she got that bruise on her hen night, there are no secrets between them. But in time there will inevitably be lows as well as highs, and when these darker times happen, it's important to focus on the reason you're together. Whenever things get tough, remember today, and everything that brought you to this moment.'

Making a marriage last: Communication is the key

Father of the bride

'Nick, I'm sure that throughout your life, wise people have assured you that as long as you communicate honestly with women and let them know what's on your mind, you'll find you have fulfilling and rewarding relationships with them. That's true to a certain extent, but I'd like to update the theory to be more specific to my daughter. By all means communicate with Anna. But remember, just like her mother, she's always right.'

Best man

'Happily married people the world over will testify that the key to a strong marriage is communication, both spoken and non-verbal. So Max, when you offer Judy a cup of tea in the morning, and all you receive is a thumbs up from under the duvet, take this as a show of her appreciation. And Judy, here's how to tell when Max is dying to kiss you. Look for the expression he was wearing in church today.'

Chief bridesmaid

'As in any marriage, communication is one of the main reasons that Simon and I are still together. On our wedding day, happily married friends and relatives all emphasized to us the importance of talking things through and thinking things over, to make our life together as strong as possible. And I can honestly say that the advice rang true: communication *is* the key, to our happy marriage. I talk and Simon listens.'

Making a marriage last
In days gone by...

Father of the bride
'In the Stone Age, Mrs Cavewoman stuck by the side of Mr Caveman for a number of reasons. These ranged from the display of virility Mr Caveman showed when he hunted and killed wild boar for dinner, to the endearing nurturing instinct Mrs Cavewoman showed when bringing cave babies into the world. But I think the real reason that marriages lasted in caveman times was because at that point no one had invented the remote control.'

Best man
'In the past, Neil would have had to woo Jessica using a combination of wit, style and cunning. He would have had to compose romantic poetry and serenade her on a nightly basis. He would have had to impress her parents with his honourable intentions, whilst displaying his waltzing prowess. Luckily for Neil, though, this is the twenty-first century, and man has a new secret weapon with which to win over a woman. Alcopops.'

Chief bridesmaid

'I'd just like to point out how lucky Bruce and Elaine are that they're not living in Victorian times. Because if they were, there would have been no living together before the wedding, and we wouldn't have Bruce's legendary performance of the Macarena to look forward to. And as for the wedding night, it's doubtful that he would have managed to remove a bodice and all those petticoats.'

Notes

Now you're buzzing with ideas to make your speech the highlight of the day. Use this space to structure what you're going to say, and then add your own anecdotes, thoughts and feelings to make your speech your own. Happy weddings!

Confetti.co.uk is the UK's leading wedding and special occasion website, helping more than 300,000 brides, grooms and guests every month.

Easy to use, the confetti.co.uk website is packed full of ideas and advice to help organize every stage of your wedding. You can choose from hundreds of beautiful wedding dresses; investigate our list of more than 3,000 wedding and reception venues; plan your wedding; chat to other brides about their experiences and ask for advice from Aunt Betti, our agony aunt. We will even help you set up a website, for you to share details and photos online with family and friends.

Our extensive online content on every aspect of weddings and special occasions is now complemented by our range of books covering every aspect of planning a wedding, for everyone involved. Titles include *Wedding Planner, Wedding Speeches, Confettiquette, Wedding Readings and Vows,* and mini books *Wedding Readings, Men At Weddings, The Best Man's Wedding, The Bridesmaid's Wedding, Your Daughter's Wedding, The Wedding Book of Calm, Compatibility* and *Wedding Trivia.*

Confetti also offer:

Wedding gifts – our exciting range, includes retro and diner furniture, homeware and accessories from Jerry's Home Store
Wedding stationery – our stunning range includes original and inspiring pieces
Wedding and party products – stocking everything you need from streamers to candles to cameras to cards to flowers to fireworks and, of course, confetti!

To find out more or to order your confetti gift book, party brochure or wedding stationery brochure:
visit: www.confetti.co.uk
call: 0870 840 6060
email: info@confetti.co.uk
visit: Confetti, 80 Tottenham Court Road, London W1